Grown-Up
Leadership

Grown-Up Leadership

The Benefits of Personal Growth
for You and Your Team

Leigh Bailey and Maureen Bailey

Available from Nova Vista Publishing:

Win-Win Selling
Vendre gagnant-gagnant (French edition of Win-Win Selling)
Versatile Selling
S'adapter à mieux vendre (French edition of Versatile Selling)
Socal Styles Handbook
I Just Love My Job!
Leading Innovation
Grown-Up Leadership
Return of the Wolf

How to order: single copies may be ordered online at www.novavistapub.com and at book stores. In North America, you may phone 503-590-8898. Elsewhere, dial +32-14-21-11-21.

ISBN 90-77256-09-1

D/2005/9797/2

Printed in Singapore

20 19 18 17 16 15 14 13 12 11 10 9 8 7 6 5 4 3 2

Editorial development: Andrew Karre
Cover design: Astrid de Deyne
Text design: Layout Sticker

CONTENTS

PART III: ACCEPTANCE AND ACTION – FOCUSING ON OTHERS

DEDICATION

It is with deep gratitude that we dedicate this book to our clients, with whom we have been honored and privileged to work over the past 16 years.

We also dedicate this book to our daughter, Allison, our greatest joy and inspiration.

ACKNOWLEDGMENTS

We want to thank the many people who were instrumental in the creation of this book.

Steve Shapiro – for his dedication, support, commitment, patience and friendship in helping us put our ideas on paper. This book would not have been possible without him.

Kathe Grooms – for being willing to take a chance on us and for being the best publishing partner we could have been given.

Allison Bailey – for her valuable editing and advice on the initial draft of the manuscript.

Dr. Priscilla Herbison and Sandra Krebs Hirsh – who had faith in us before we had faith in ourselves and lovingly fostered our growth and development over these many years.

David Haben, Ruth Hayden and Barb Krantz Taylor, and many others – who read and offered advice during the early development of the manuscript.

And to all the people who have supported us in our development journeys – who are too many to list but to whom we are profoundly grateful.

MAUREEN BAILEY AND LEIGH BAILEY

FOREWORD

It's a pleasure to welcome you to the world of *Grown-Up Leadership*. I've known Leigh and Maureen Bailey and admired the fruits of their work for 16 years. I'm delighted to see them use their exceptional integrity, common sense, congeniality, and wisdom as they share their insights and practical experience to write, in easy-to-understand (yet hard-to-practice) terms, about what is required to be a truly great leader.

The Baileys address the key challenges 21st-century managers face – how to build relationships with, motivate, and retain workers; plus how to align everyone's know-how and energy to drive innovation, creative problem solving, and superior financial results.

They have an impressive ability to translate leadership theories and concepts into practical methods for personal development and leadership growth. In their work with clients, they have helped many high-potential performers move from being great at tasks to becoming great leaders who get things done through others. They also exemplify the grown-up leadership traits they describe in this book. Think of them as your personal coaches, talking to you in stereo.

Leigh and Maureen's method requires authenticity and personal maturity – the maturity that seeks to know oneself, to adapt to different types of people while staying true to one's own core, to have the personal discipline to make changes and follow through with them, and to practice the versatility required in today's organizations.

The book is based on real-life insights and experience derived from the hundreds of executives who have had the good fortune to work with the Baileys. If you practice its wisdom, you will benefit not just yourself as a leader, but your team and organization too.

Writers in writing classes are often given the advice to write about what they know. Leigh and Maureen Bailey have done just that in this book – so read it, put it to work, and share it with those who will benefit from adopting a *Grown-Up Leadership* style!

SANDRA KREBS HIRSH
Consultant and Author of LIFETypes and other titles

TEACHING AND LEARNING
ABOUT LEADERSHIP

No leader is ever fully realized. At most, one can observe individuals who are in the course of attaining greater skills and heightened effectiveness.

HOWARD GARDNER

Many leaders are praised for being bottom-line driven – working to achieve success at any cost. But they also leave behind a trail of unhappy employees, motivated by fear and more focused on finding their next job than on improving their performance. Leaders who fail to bring maturity to their day-to-day work cannot succeed in the long run, because they continually alienate people. They are dinosaurs in today's business world.

In our work as leadership coaches, we have observed many qualities and skills that contribute to effective leadership. Foremost among them is a level of self-awareness and maturity that comes as a result of commitment to personal development. Not every leader buys into the link between enlightenment and business. But we have seen hundreds of cases where leaders' failures to grow up – which keep them stuck in habitual, reactive behavior based on childhood or family-based demons – prevent them from achieving their business objectives.

In our view, the 21st century's business world challenges leaders to be masters in the art of human development. As a leader, you must assess your own abilities and seek out tools that specifically enhance your personal development. That's where we come in, as leadership coaches. By supporting the *personal* growth of our clients, we help them address their leadership challenges. We see, in the results of our holistic approach to leadership, changes in our clients' lives that give them their best chances of success today. We therefore encourage you to actively use this book to help you examine yourself, and to develop yourself further in ways that support your success as a leader.

We believe that the key ingredients for exceptional leadership include:

- Maturity: the courage to develop self-awareness and understanding, and to make changes when you discover personal barriers.
- Versatility: the ability to understand and learn other leadership styles.
- Relationship-building ability: the willingness to engage others to get results.

When leaders have these assets, they become great coaches and team-builders.

In the coming pages, we will examine leadership in many ways, but most importantly as it influences the behavior of others. Being grown up takes you a long way toward leading effectively. That may seem obvious, yet it continually amazes us to hear how many leaders act childishly. Putting it bluntly, people deserve grown-up leaders! We aim to give you the skills and abilities we've seen in the best leaders among us, to help you join that group.

THE CHARACTERISTICS OF GREAT LEADERS

In our consulting practice, we have worked with literally thousands of leaders from small organizations all the way up to Fortune 100 corporate executives. We regularly ask ourselves what characterizes the best leaders we have met. The qualities we have identified among these top leaders constitute the core concepts of this book:

- They have become aware of their fears and anxieties and are no longer driven by them, having taken the time and energy to really know and accept themselves. In the process, they have developed the ability to adapt their natural styles when situations require it. That's a growing-up process, one that requires real commitment and hard work, but which leads to real *maturity*.
- They have pushed themselves beyond their natural leadership styles to learn and practice different (and at first, uncomfortable) techniques. This *versatility* gives them greater capacity for guiding, influencing, and understanding.
- They recognize the importance of achieving results and objectives through the people they work with, and invest in *relationship-building and coaching* with their employees, making personal connections that inspire trust and motivate others to do their best work.
- They are sophisticated about *teamwork*, particularly about how their role as leader affects group dynamics.

In our practice, we have developed a new vocabulary to talk about leadership. We often are asked to coach high potential leaders who are not leading well, sometimes as part of a crisis intervention to prevent dismissal. We help our clients find *mindful* ways to address their leadership shortcomings and permanently enhance their effectiveness. As you read on, we will continually encourage you to expand your notion of what qualities contribute to effective leadership, and to examine your own experiences and beliefs about leadership that may be getting in the way of your success as a leader.

SITTING AT THE GROWN-UP TABLE

We named this book *Grown-Up Leadership* partly because for us, it conjures up images of giant family dinners. Adults typically sit at the grown-up table in the dining room, while young children are relegated to a table in the kitchen or family room. To be invited to sit with the grownups is an honor, but it also requires good manners. Childish behavior is not tolerated at the grown-up table.

The concept of being grown up, then, means letting go of childish behavior. No pinching, unscrewing the caps of salt and pepper shakers, or throwing food at your cousins!

This metaphor works because, in fact, some leaders among us still act like they're sitting at the kids' table. They lose control of their emotions, keep their "me-first" mentality, bully others, or act dishonestly. If we don't tolerate such behavior at the grown-up table at home, why should we tolerate it among our leaders?

Think about how hard it is to be around adults who still act in childish ways. Then imagine how hard it is to have a boss who behaves immaturely. It's a nightmare: you feel frustrated, demotivated, and may look for another job. In contrast, working for a grown-up boss can be a dream: you give your very best and feel fulfilled and appreciated. But make no mistake – leaders who are grownups have worked hard to mature into healthy individuals. They have learned how to manage relationships with others, can make workplaces feel positive, and motivate employees to increase productivity.

WHAT DOES – AND DOESN'T – WORK

Based on our experience, organizations that encourage their leaders to become grown-up human beings see bottom-line results. Leaders who have a healthy sense of self-worth, a strong curiosity about people and things, and an acute awareness of both their own and others' feelings – all qualities of maturity – succeed by actively engaging employees, establishing creative and productive work environments, and achieving boardroom objectives as well.

In the course of this book, we will take you through a progression of discussions and exercises that will help you to develop yourself, but then also help you direct your leadership skills to people you lead, coaching

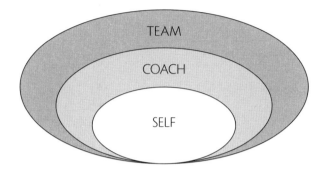

THE RIPPLE EFFECT OF GROWN-UP LEADERSHIP

TEAM

COACH

SELF

Our experience shows that you must first come to know and accept yourself in order to be truly effective coaching your employees and leading teams.

them to be their best. We will give you insights and tips that will help you get the best out of teams, as well. The ripple effect, radiating out from your work on yourself, will be evident throughout our discussions.

But you may be wondering: What about organizations that have not come to recognize the importance of grown-up leadership? In our experience, they continue to hire people at key leadership levels who are stuck in immature behavior patterns that sabotage their missions and make people leave. Believe us – we have worked with many leaders who:

- Procrastinate
- Feel crushed by their workload
- Appear unable to connect with their co-workers
- Struggle to contain their anger or frustration at co-workers
- Act like they know it all, but confide to us that they secretly believe they are imposters
- Are jealous of the successes of their co-workers and employees
- Are unable to sustain meaningful, trusting relationships with colleagues

Employees should not have to deal with such immature behavior.

> Be not afraid of growing slowly, be afraid only of standing still.
> CHINESE PROVERB

Leadership requires outgrowing such immaturity and gaining the skills required to sit at the grown-up table. Getting in touch with your insides, and learning to observe your own actions and behavior with curiosity and objectivity, will help you gain the capacity you need to make the kind of changes that great leaders make. Such self-awareness can be painful at first, but will translate into results that you, your employees, your peers, and your superiors will definitely notice.

A MODEL FOR CHANGE

The sum of your personal beliefs, which stems from your lifetime of experiences and relationships, creates a personal prism through which you view the world. These beliefs directly affect your everyday thoughts and emotions, both in your personal and professional lives. But many of these beliefs are unexamined, even unconscious, and you may not perceive their impact. With hard work, as you gain insight into these unconscious beliefs, you can better understand the causes of the thoughts and emotions that keep you from achieving your objectives.

Real, lasting change is gradual, a process rather than an event. The change process requires learning about your beliefs and taking steps to overcome those that have become barriers in your life. We use a personal change model with our clients that has roots in both 12-Step programs (like Al-Anon), and in Zen Buddhism: we call it Awareness-Acceptance-Action. The most successful of our clients – particularly those who make changes in their lives and then sustain them – follow this model for change.

AWARENESS: AWAKENING AND LEARNING

Many who choose to lead are high achievers – individuals who push themselves to accomplish, who strive for personal excellence. Some

THE AWARENESS-ACCEPTANCE-ACTION (AAA) CHANGE MODEL

We picture the AAA Change Model as a looping line that moves you forward. It suggests your movement inward (and, many say, downward!) as you first seek *awareness*. Then, in the *acceptance* stage, you apply determination and gain perspective on yourself. That enables you to invest energy and move forward and upward as you take *action* in your change-making stage.

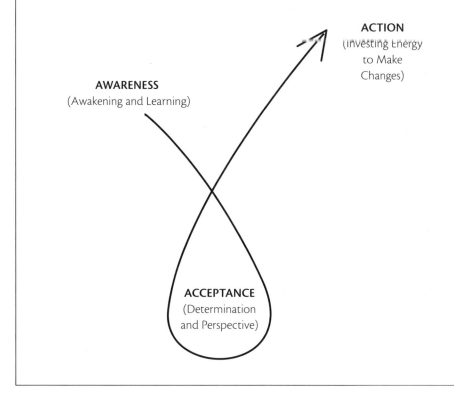

ACTION
(Investing Energy
to Make
Changes)

AWARENESS
(Awakening and Learning)

ACCEPTANCE
(Determination
and Perspective)

even become compulsive in their pursuit of achievement. But when high achievers are confronted with their deficiencies, and begin to learn how those deficiencies contribute to their shortcomings as leaders, their motivation to achieve often turns into unnecessarily harsh self-criticism. Through *Awareness* we learn about our own behaviors, awakening to aspects of ourselves that were previously hidden from us. As our eyes open, we begin to gain more perspective on our own behavior.

ACCEPTANCE: DETERMINATION AND PERSPECTIVE

Acceptance, the second stage of our change model, helps us become gentler with ourselves by teaching us to detach, step back, and look at our issues more objectively. We begin to move beyond embarrassment and guilt, and to gradually realize that there are more productive alternatives to our troublesome behaviors. By becoming more skillful at self-observation and recognizing choices we can make, we see how outmoded behavior keeps us from being our best selves. More importantly, we start to learn how we can change.

Acceptance means becoming less embarrassed about old behaviors, and instead, growing curious about them. Success in this stage requires that you develop personal persistence to learn more about yourself, your beliefs and your actions. When you find a loose thread of information, you can push yourself to learn how that thread has run through your life. During the acceptance stage, you might also risk becoming more personally revealing, confiding and then exploring your discoveries with others. The rewards can be amazingly rich.

ACTION: INVESTING ENERGY TO MAKE CHANGES

At work, acceptance often makes us realize that sometimes, old behaviors keep us from achieving our objectives. It's time to commit to investigating them, then to learn other ways of behaving and break those old, ineffective habits. As we start to experiment with new behaviors, we will develop strategies to enhance strengths and to deal with weaknesses. In short, we start to take *Action* to grow up as individuals and as leaders.

Action goes well beyond learning about yourself. At some point, you can learn only so much, ponder new options, examine old behaviors, and think about situations differently. Action requires the energy to do something new, to experiment with new behaviors, and to consider changes from the inside out.

The *Awareness-Acceptance-Action* model (AAA) is more than just a thinking process. It requires you to actively set new goals, consciously seek out ways to behave differently with others, acknowledge discomfort, and use your energy to take new risks to continue on your course. People who emerge from the AAA process make *real* changes in their work, careers and lives. When we learn, think, and act mindfully instead of habitually, we gain confidence and achieve results. Only then can we begin to create and sustain really productive individual and team relationships.

MEET THE ACCOMMODATOR AND THE INTIMIDATOR

Our process also recognizes that there are different *types* of people, whose styles look dramatically different in leadership positions. Most individuals lean in one of two directions. One is a compliant person, who is comfortable with an empowering approach. That's the Accommodator. The other is a more aggressive person, who tends to use a forceful approach. That's the Intimidator. Both of these styles or tendencies result from your upbringing, experiences and preferences.

As you work through the chapters of this book, we will help you understand your own behavioral tendencies and personal style. To help illustrate how these contrasting styles function in the workplace, we will share stories of Neil (an Accommodator) and Marilyn (an Intimidator), two leaders who are trying to make personal and professional changes in order to become more effective in their work. While they are not real individuals, they are based on numerous people we work with who face real-world challenges. As you follow their stories, you will gain insight into their behaviors and watch them grow up, combining self-knowledge and new skills to give themselves useful new leadership tools.

Although in most of this book we speak in a single authorial voice, it happens that we also represent these two types: Leigh is an Accommodator, Maureen an Intimidator. So in the *He Says/She Says* boxes you

ACCOMMODATORS AND INTIMIDATORS

Leigh Says

As an Accommodator, I typically try to consider the needs of others before I act. I play by the rules, tend to seek the approval of others around me, and avoid confrontation whenever possible. As a leader, I try to empower others to act: I prefer to see them rather than myself in the limelight.

HE SHE SAYS

Maureen Says

As an Intimidator, I don't hesitate to share my ideas and opinions, sometimes blurting them out, interrupting, or speaking over others. I am comfortable standing up for what I believe, and can challenge others who disagree with me. As a leader, I tend to prefer a forceful style, which feels direct and clean to me.

will see from time to time, we'll give you our personal perspectives from these orientations, to help you see more clearly what these tendencies imply.

What results can you expect from investing in this development process? When working with our clients, we try to help them measure success in small accomplishments, gradually building up a history of awareness and action using the AAA change model. Over time, leaders report that these small successes start to have big impacts. Read on, work hard, and you'll begin to recognize that these are the moments of transition into grown-up leadership.

How to use this book as your personal coach

We have organized this book so that you can experience the typical sequence of coaching and consulting we follow with our clients. You can therefore use it as a self-development guide. However, we do not intend for it to *replace* the work that you can do with a professional coach. Rather, it will introduce you to concepts and help you begin the personal growth process that can improve your leadership capacity.

Each chapter concludes with a set of *Driving Principles*, a set of bullet-pointed thoughts that distill the most critical points from that chapter. We intend these both as summaries and as exclamation points – as you move forward, you might use these as review points or even daily affirmations to reinforce our discussions on grown-up leadership.

You will also find a section at the end of each chapter called *Your Personal Coaching Session*. It will lead you through the Awareness-Acceptance-Action process. This process, starting with learning about your beliefs, through coming to terms with them, and moving on to planning and taking action steps, has helped many of our clients overcome major barriers to their professional success.

We admire the work of many academics and professionals who came before us, and regularly incorporate many of their ideas into our work. In particular, we are indebted to the influences of Carl Rogers, Abraham Maslow, Carl Jung, Albert Ellis, Pema Chödrön, Karen Horney, Jim Collins, Robert Kaplan, Clayton Lafferty, Daniel Goleman and Isabel Myers. You will find entries about their major works, and other key readings, in our bibliography. But now, let's get started.

PART I

AWARENESS AND ACCEPTANCE

Never in the history of humankind
have we had so many means of communication,
yet we remain islands.

THICH NHAT HANH

CHAPTER ONE

PATHS TO GROWN-UP LEADERSHIP

Nobody dreams of being a poor leader. In our combined 30 years of coaching and consulting, we can say with absolute certainty that no one intentionally begins their day saying, "Today I'm going to be a poor leader and frustrate, confuse, and demoralize my valued staff."

Nevertheless, most of us can recall managers we have known or worked for who were indecisive, power-hungry, narrow-minded, glory-seeking, or in other ways immature and ineffective. The fact that bad leaders are so common underscores the fact that leading well is a challenge, and that effective leadership is a scarce resource in most organizations. Certainly there are leaders who have wonderful, natural leadership traits. They inspire others with their vision, express themselves clearly, build consensus, and gain the trust and commitment of colleagues and employees. Through others, they get results.

Most of us, however, have not been blessed with *all* these gifts of leadership. We are burdened with unexamined and imperfect lessons from our pasts that preserve old fears, insecurities and insufficient self-awareness. The result of this historical baggage is that, though we may not set out to be ineffective leaders, we often unintentionally confuse and frustrate our employees and fail to provide the direction and inspiration our followers seek – and deserve.

What makes leadership difficult? Effective leadership requires more than mastering tasks. Those who are skilled with numbers, electronics, design, sales, or organization demonstrate the capacity to be successful *workers*. But if you aspire to be effective as a leader, the ability to complete a task is not enough. Success as a leader requires accomplishing tasks through other people. This requires you to be highly skilled in managing yourself and your relations with others. This blend of human qualities, personal insight, learned abilities, and focused effort is one we will investigate in the following chapters. It is how we define "growing up."

ACCOMPLISHING THINGS THROUGH OTHERS

To illustrate the importance of accomplishing tasks through other people, let's consider some examples of leadership that we hear about every day:

- Football fans judge a coach's performance by the results of the team on the field. The head coach doesn't play on the field, but rather works from the sidelines. He can do his best to prepare his team, put the right people into the right positions, encourage them to perform at their best, and call the plays that will yield the best outcome. But ultimately he can only watch.
- A director of a play oversees casting, set design, lighting, and works methodically during rehearsals to translate her vision into a successful show. But once the house lights go out and the performance begins, she must stand offstage and watch her actors perform for the audience.

These leaders realize that they need to reach objectives that have been set out in advance: winning the game or giving the audience a good show. Their success relies on others who understand their roles, share a vision, and commit to following the path that the leader articulates. It's easier to see this in sports or the theater, harder in the business world. But the concept is the same.

In short, effective leaders hire, train, motivate, and inspire others. They know how to identify the needs of people they manage, and determine the best ways to relate to them, both one-on-one and as a team. And they have the courage and confidence to confront poor performance or ineffective behavior, and to remove individuals who are harmful to their organizations. Effectiveness in this realm goes well beyond using one's natural leadership tendencies: it requires a conscious commitment to personal and professional growth. When you see a good leader, almost certainly you are seeing a person with some natural gifts – who has also worked hard to bring them up to top form. That's what we want to do with you in the course of this book.

FEAR AND ANXIETY

Great leadership requires certain skills that can only be learned through hard work. Specifically, you need honesty, courage and the ability to examine your fears and anxieties objectively. Fear and anxiety are two major barriers to effective leadership. They keep us from taking risks, proposing new ideas, initiating innovative projects or trying to master new skills. But as humans, we all struggle with personal issues. How do some of us overcome them better than others?

> We cannot solve our problems with the same thinking we used when we created them.
>
> ALBERT EINSTEIN

As we will discuss in considerable depth, becoming more aware of the beliefs that underlie your approach to leadership is an important step in growing up as a leader. Leaders who want to grow need to learn to become active participants in their own success. Experience gives us the "gray hair" that people trust in a leader. But experience without learning and reflection can foster narrow thinking and a limited world view.

Let's take an example of the limitations of experience alone. Suppose you grew up in a home with highly intelligent parents. Perhaps you found that debating with your parents was frustrating and discouraging, because they always seemed to know more than you about whatever subject you were discussing. Eventually you learned to keep quiet and go along with your parent's opinions, even if you disagreed, to avoid the pain of being ignored or misunderstood.

Now, fast forward to your promotion to become new CEO of a manufacturing firm. The previous CEO has remained involved in the business as an advisor and part owner. You want to build your own leadership team, which will require firing employees from the previous regime. When you talk about this with the former CEO, she reminds you that you are new to your job and suggests that you will benefit from the experience of her team members. You are confronted with a gut-wrenching choice: Do you keep quiet and go along with the former CEO's advice, or trust your own opinion and move forward with the changes, at the risk of inciting the anger of your former boss? How will your experience with your parents influence your choice?

> [O]ur hang-ups, unfortunately or fortunately, contain our wealth. Our neurosis and our wisdom are made out of the same material. If you throw out your neurosis, you also throw out your wisdom. The idea isn't to try to get rid of your [weakness], but to make friends with it, to see it clearly with precision and honesty, and also to see it with gentleness.
>
> PEMA CHÖDRÖN

LEADERS AS LEARNERS

As we said earlier, becoming aware of the beliefs underlying your approach to leadership is central to your growth as a leader. This learning process requires a new approach to learning, self-awareness and change. In our practice, we observe that many leaders erroneously believe the most efficient path to their growth and development is through self-criticism – a short-term solution at best. They often become discouraged when they try to use self-criticism and will power to change their ineffective behavior. They bear down on their weaknesses, and maybe make some short-term progress, only to find themselves quickly reverting to old habits. As a result, when they discover a weakness or blind spot in themselves, they feel ashamed or embarrassed about their discovery, and try to hide their weaknesses from themselves and others.

Lasting personal change requires a more extensive learning process. That's why we work to help people move beyond simple, aggressive self-criticism into self-acceptance. Our recipe for deep and enduring change is built on the following principles:

- Change begins with awareness.
- Change takes time and can be uncomfortable.
- Self-observation and feedback provide necessary data for making skillful behavioral changes that will endure.
- Change requires the support of others; it is difficult (perhaps impossible) to grow significantly without enlisting the help of others.
- Being gentle and patient with yourself is, paradoxically, the most efficient and effective path to long-term, sustainable change.

The majority of leaders we have coached initially resist this new approach to learning and change, asking, "How can being gentle and patient get results?" It's enigmatic advice, we agree – and it's advice that's very, very hard to accept and put into action. However, even with our most resistant clients, we have found that if they remain open to this process and give it their best effort, they experience radical, positive transformation in their effectiveness as leaders.

CONVERTING INSIGHT INTO ACTION

New behaviors feel uncomfortable: we typically feel insecure, incapable, or slightly out-of-whack when first trying something new. Fear of the unknown, in fact, is enough of a barrier to keep many of us stuck in damaging behavior. Yet thanks to our work with many clients, we are convinced that habitual, defensive, fear-based behavior is almost always at the root of failed leadership. Conversely, leaders who succeed in the long term have mastered the principles of sustainable personal change, and have learned to apply them to support their own and their employees' development.

We hold that there is no single model of effective leadership, but rather a set of underlying principles common to successful leadership models. Learning these principles is vital for leaders at all levels, particularly for those aspiring to senior leadership positions. Successful leaders continually study how other leaders – both historical and modern – have succeeded and failed. They develop their own capacity for growth. They work on becoming more personally conscious of their own habitual, often ineffective and outdated defense mechanisms, and commit to trying new behaviors that work better in today's new circumstances. They become both more accepting and more demanding of themselves and of others, as they seek to lead their teams towards new levels of success and accomplishments. That's because they believe that *acceptance* and *challenge* are key ingredients to healthy, productive work environments. Under these conditions, leaders and workers alike perform better, are more willing to take risks, and produce better bottom-line results.

> Our ability to grow is directly proportional to an ability to entertain the uncomfortable.
> TWYLA THARP

DRIVING PRINCIPLES

- Leaders must master relationship skills, as well as technical skills, to achieve long-term success.
- Leaders must be aware of and consciously manage their belief systems and behavior in order to be most effective.
- Leaders who are effective over time have mastered the principles of sustainable personal change, and have learned to apply them in support of their own and their employees' learning and development.

Your Personal Coaching Session

Sharing Leadership Challenges

Recently, we worked with a group of managers in a large organization. We asked them to discuss some of the barriers that they faced as leaders. With some modifications, their responses were typical of the individuals and groups we work with. They shared these specific challenges:

- Managing work flow through both busy and slow times
- Defining roles for people and making room for them to grow
- Thinking about the future and articulating their vision
- Balancing performance of tasks vs. building relationships
- Doing the work themselves vs. taking the time to coach and develop their staff
- Maintaining a focus on both daily work and the big picture
- Handling staff changes
- Saying no to a client or co-worker
- Prioritizing lists of tasks and activities

To expand leadership abilities, we encourage clients to identify and discuss leadership challenges with trusted associates. Sharing opens up a resource of rich ideas and real world experiences. Asking a colleague: "How would you handle this problem?" is taking a very positive first step.

So here's your task: make a list of issues you face as a leader. Be as specific as possible. For example, instead of simply saying "employee difficulties," write "How should I handle problems with Joe's attitude towards co-workers?" Choose an individual you trust, and schedule some time to share the items on your list with them. Open your mind to the person's feedback and ideas.

Afterward, evaluate the experience. Did you get a richer pool of options, insights, key facts? Would it be worthwhile to do this more often?

The contents of our unconscious
are constantly being projected
into our surroundings.

CARL JUNG

CHAPTER TWO

OVERCOMING PERSONAL BARRIERS

In Chapter One we focused on self-awareness and argued that it is critical to your development as a leader. Let's expand on this idea now.

Every person has a unique set of talents, gifts, and blind spots, the result of innate personality and a lifetime of experiences. We believe that leaders who are really aware of their strengths and weaknesses – and who base their actions on that awareness – are ultimately more successful as leaders.

Few things are true of all of us, except this: we all are human. As humans, we carry a lifetime of experiences in our memories, dating back to early childhood. These include experiences with parents and caregivers, siblings, friends, schools, religious institutions, and countless other sources of influence. Experiences influence our beliefs, the way we respond to outside stimuli, and certainly, the way we relate to others.

Strangely enough, though, many leaders we've worked with have a hard time accepting that their life history affects their ability to lead others. Yet the person each of us is today is the sum of our genetic inheritance and life history. And it's impossible to separate our private selves from our working selves.

Nevertheless, we are convinced that there is a definite, predictable link between our human development and our capacity to lead. Experiences from childhood to today affect our performance. As we see it, our ability to become more aware of the ways in which our past affects us is a key opportunity for growth.

Take a simple example. When you see a dog walking down the street, will you treat it as a potential friend or foe? That probably depends on your experience with dogs as a child. There's a big difference between considering dogs as beloved pets and considering dogs to be like that scary hound next door that you used to avoid at all costs. Whatever you learned as a child, you can expect that your action – whether to approach the dog or avoid it – will be based on the internal message you received from your earlier experience, *unless you consciously decide to act differently.*

Here's a work example: early in your career you initiated a high-risk project that did not pan out. As a result, you were harshly criticized and ultimately fired. Even if that experience took place many years ago, it may still affect the way you respond to the perceived risk of a new idea or initiative. For example, you may unthinkingly react negatively to a particularly entrepreneurial proposal from a subordinate, based on your past experience, rather than objectively examining the details of the particular idea.

Let's flip that example around for a moment. Imagine you are an employee with a great new idea and you are presenting it to your boss for approval. How would your morale, self-esteem, or motivation be affected if you knew your boss reacted to the idea based more on his previous experiences than on the specific merits of your proposal? How could this action affect your overall productivity?

RECOGNIZING THE POWER OF PERCEPTION

So, much as it pains most of us to admit it, life experience – and family experience – impact the ways we act as leaders in the workplace. Most work situations are hierarchical systems. As such, they are fertile grounds that reactivate our old beliefs, values, issues with authority, and concerns regarding self-esteem and self-worth.

Let's consider, for example, the approval-seeking nature of most work environments. Early in our careers, we must seek approval from others (particularly superiors) in order to make a place for ourselves and to be noticed for future promotions. This normal approval-seeking process echoes experiences with parents and other authority figures from the past, and unresolved resentments and fears from childhood can resurface as a result. Leaders willing to look at these life experiences will have greater awareness of how to respond when old feelings are reignited.

If this sounds like a psychology primer, then you are starting to grasp the link we make between your personal development experiences (your psychological development) and your growth as a leader.

In this area, we appreciate the work of Albert Ellis, a prominent expert in cognitive-behavioral psychology, who was a pioneer in understanding the connection between past experience and present behavior. His findings have consistently enlightened our work with leaders. Ellis studied the process of connecting inside beliefs with outside events in an effort to gain insight into why people think, feel, and behave as they do in certain situations. According to Ellis, the process starts with A, an *activating event*, or an everyday occurrence that we respond to – like an encounter with a co-worker, a traffic incident, or an unexpected phone call.

We react to these events, Ellis suggests, through B, a set of *beliefs* that affects how we see the world: our own unique collection of history and experiences. Think of this belief system as a prism through which we view the world. This personal prism affects our vision, and the prism, rather than the activating events in our lives, affects C, the *consequences* of a given interaction, specifically our thinking, our emotional response, and especially our behavior. According to Ellis, the way we act – in life, in relationships, and in work situations – is based on this A-B-C Model.

ALBERT ELLIS' STRUCTURE OF INTERPRETATION (ABC MODEL)

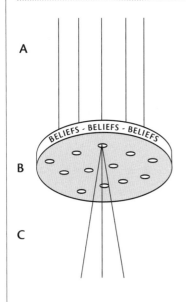

Activating Events (A)

Outside events that we respond to daily.

Beliefs (B)

The belief systems through which we filter Activating Events. These systems spring from our unique collection of genetic inheritance and experience. Our beliefs can be either rational or irrational.

Consequences (C)

The internal and external consequences of A and B: how we think, feel and behave in response to those activating events.

A story we heard from Larry Wilson at Wilson Learning Center illuminates this concept. Imagine three people who grew up in Florida, USA, are sitting in a room: one person grew up in the Everglades and kept snakes for pets; the second grew up in Miami, was bitten once by a poisonous snake, and nearly died; and the third person grew up in Tampa and only had experience with harmless snakes. If you walk into the room carrying a twelve-foot boa constrictor wrapped around your shoulders (a farfetched idea, we admit), how do you imagine each person might respond? Why would the three people react differently?

> Whether you believe you can do a thing or not, you're right.
> HENRY FORD

Like Ellis and many others, we believe our past personal experiences and the resulting beliefs we have formed (which we may not even be aware of) affect our daily lives, in and out of work. Clearly, we don't all respond to activating events in the same way. As leaders, it is our beliefs, which act as mediators between activating events and the resulting consequences, that are central to our overall leadership effectiveness. And if we study a group of leaders, we notice that there are considerable differences between the beliefs of the effective and ineffective leaders among them.

Here's the rub. Many beliefs, especially those developed as ways of coping with perceived threats to our personal safety and self-esteem in the past, have outlived their usefulness. When our daughter was three, we taught her never to go out into the street unless she was holding an adult's hand. We can recall numerous times during her childhood when she stayed out of harm's way because she followed that rule. Now, let's imagine she never consciously examined the usefulness of that rule as an adult. That would mean that she would still look for hands to hold when crossing the street, even though she's now in her twenties.

> What we believe about ourselves can hold us hostage...We do not see things as they are...we see them as WE are.
>
> RACHEL NAOMI REMEN

Though that might seem silly, we regularly meet people in leadership positions who continue to apply childhood rules (or habits) that have long since outlived their usefulness. These habitual, protective responses can be hurtful, destructive and ineffective, and tend to override healthy leadership responses. When we react out of habit, we reduce the likelihood that we'll accomplish our present-day objectives.

All of us keep core beliefs about the world and about behavior in our heads. These beliefs might apply to eating, sleeping, asking for help, interacting with others, taking risks, handling money, or exploring new ideas. If we don't challenge beliefs that are no longer relevant to our lives, then we will become limited in our capacity to act appropriately in new situations.

There are many ways in which you can gain insight into how you perceive your world. Recognizing the prism through which you look is an important starting point for transforming your personal awareness and effectiveness. We will discuss other approaches in upcoming chapters.

BECOMING CONSCIOUS OF YOUR UNCONSCIOUS

The difficult journey through the land of self-examination takes great courage. Many people feel quite uncomfortable when they start to learn about themselves, either through self-examination or through some unexpected feedback from a co-worker or friend. They feel exposed, child-like, and often, ashamed. Letting go of habitual, protective behaviors is like going into a battle without armor, and that's a scary notion.

> There is always a choice about the way you do your work, even if there is not a choice about the work itself.
>
> LUNDIN, PAUL, AND CHRISTENSEN

But this process offers many rewards as well. In the 1960s, Abraham Maslow popularized the concept of *self-actualization*, which he defined as having a healthy sense of self-worth and self-trust, a strong curiosity about people, and an acute awareness of both one's own and others' thoughts and feelings. We call this process "growing up." The process of maturing as a human being requires an inside-out examination of one's belief system, revisiting old memories, pondering past experiences, examining relationships, and gaining insight into the filter or prism through which one views outside experiences. Those who can navigate this process will gain new tools that will help them lead others effectively.

Ultimately the process of maturing is a barrier for many. They resist the notion that personal growth is a prerequisite for professional growth. But in our experience, leaders with the most resistance to this course of action are actually the ones with the greatest need for it. Those who view the world through an unexamined filter tend to be more negative, narrow-minded, aggressive, short-sighted, and critical, *or*, conversely, they are excessively passive, fearful, or indecisive. In short, they rely on old survival tools such as intimidation, micro-managing, hogging credit, or withdrawal – behaviors that aren't very productive in business.

Becoming aware of your beliefs enables you to begin to adjust thinking styles and substantially change outcomes. Leaders with this level of awareness show a greater sense of confidence and competence than oth-

BIRTH ORDER AS A LEARNING TOOL

Recent research on the birth order of children within family units has yielded interesting findings that pertain to leadership. The studies confirm our common sense observations and identify specific tendencies in roles that oldest, middle and youngest children play in conflicts, crises – or in workplace group dynamics.

* Oldest children, or first-borns, are most likely to be the ones that take charge in group situations. They define tasks, assign roles and tend to lead groups they participate in.

* Middle children tend to be the peacemakers and diplomats in our midst. In groups, they try to make sure that everyone feels included, connected, and satisfied with their role.

* Youngest, or last-born children, are often the playful ones among us. They seek to make friends with people, and are often the quiet rule-breakers of the group.

There are certainly many exceptions to these factors that complicate general tendencies, like culture, gender, or present age, but we are often surprised by how valid and applicable they are as tools for looking at people.

Source: Paul Vaughn, Educational Consultant, Educational Early Start

ers do. Learning about – and overcoming – sources of fear and anxiety in your life gives you more inner joy, peacefulness, and security. Most of all, if you have this awareness, you develop greater inner resources. Your actions and personal feelings are driven by your internal values and core beliefs, rather than a need for acceptance or recognition from others.

DRIVING PRINCIPLES
* There's a definite link between aspects of growing up and your capacity to lead.

- Unconscious beliefs have a dramatic effect on your conscious behavior.
- Your behavior in certain situations is more dependent on your own interpretation of events than on the event itself.

Your Personal Coaching Session

Exploring Your Personal Prism

Gaining insight about the filter through which you view the world will help you in your own development as a leader. It helps to think of a prism: when you shine a light through it, the prism breaks the light up into the spectrum of colors, from red to green to violet. The prism helps you see those colors clearly, even though they aren't typically visible to the naked eye.

Use the metaphor of the prism to examine your system of personal beliefs. The process requires looking at all the life experiences that have influenced you to better understand how you perceive the world.

In this exercise, you will begin gathering data about early influences and experiences that can be processed as we continue through this book together. To do it, you will need a quiet, comfortable place to write, a notebook, and your favorite pen.

STEP ONE: PERSONAL HISTORY

Take a few minutes to write answers to the questions below about your personal history. Like the colors of the spectrum, these topics collectively contribute to the way you filter information, and affect how you think, feel and behave at work and in the rest of your life. It's best if you really focus on these questions one by one, pause, and then write a few words to capture your thoughts. If you prefer, you might have a trusted friend or colleague ask the questions and write down your responses for you.

Birth
- Where were you born?

Your Personal Coaching Session
(continued)

- How would you describe the kind of community (i.e., city, small town, farm) where you grew up?
- How would you describe the family you were born into?

Work

- Which members of your family worked during your childhood? How much?
- Did they like their work? Did they have a sense of purpose? Were they successful?
- What early messages did you receive from your family about work?

Siblings

- Are you an only child or do you have siblings? If you have siblings, where were you in the birth order of your family?
- What roles did you play in your relationships with your siblings, if any (e.g., leader, peacemaker, attention-getter, trouble maker)? If you are an only child, how did that fact shape your behavior as a child?
- In what ways do you play the same role(s) as an adult?

Authority

- Who was in charge in your family?
- How would you describe their leadership style?
- What other authority figures (e.g., teachers, coaches, neighbors) played significant roles in your childhood? What impacts did they have?

Values

- Who were some individuals or institutions that your family members liked, respected or admired?
- What types of people did your family members criticize?
- Were family members optimistic or pessimistic? How did that affect your beliefs or behavior?

Religion

- What role did religion play in your upbringing?
- What beliefs about religion affect your behavior?

Financial

- What role did money play in your family?
- How were financial issues discussed?
- Who had input into financial decisions?

Temperament and emotions

- What emotions were visible or tolerated in your family? What emotions were not visible or tolerated? By whom?
- When thinking about your childhood, what emotions do you recall most strongly?
- How did others describe you as a child?

Conflict

- What happened when people disagreed in your family?
- Was conflict encouraged, discouraged or tolerated?

Nurturing

- What was the safest way for you to express a need, desire, idea, or goal as a child?
- Who was the most likely to support what you asked for?
- How did you get your emotional needs met?

STEP TWO: REFLECTION

Take a few minutes with coffee, tea or anything that will help put you in the mood for quiet thinking. Review the questions and your answers one by one. Try to identify the insights you gained as you answered the questions. Are there any people you'd like to talk with to further explore your personal prism? Use any means of creative expression that feels appropriate to capture your thoughts. Save these for your future work.

It takes more courage to reveal insecurities than to hide them,
more strength to relate to people than to dominate them ...
to abide by thought-out principles rather than blind reflex.

A. KARRAS

CHAPTER THREE

TURN AND LOOK

Being grown up is important for all adults, but it's a vital trait in an outstanding leader. While people grow and mature differently, those who strive to become great leaders need to recognize situations in life that offer opportunities for learning about themselves. Choosing to become aware of your personal belief systems requires you to examine the anxieties and fears that accompany them, and to respond consciously rather than react to outside stimuli out of habit. We call this process "Turn and Look."

Don't be fooled: being grown up does not require perfection. In fact, as you gain maturity, you will recognize and accept your own imperfections and the limitations of others. This process – becoming more aware of our imperfections – is often humbling. But as you will see, such self-examination is extremely valuable to you as a leader.

This chapter focuses on the relationship between ineffective leadership and unexamined beliefs. Leaders whose actions are affected by personal fears and anxieties can seem petty, judgmental, inconsistent, and even immature to their co-workers. Such behavior is the result of old, comfortable, yet destructive habits. To overcome these habits, you must try new behaviors, which can make you feel unsure, insecure and vulnerable – at least at the start.

Consider this example. A new CEO that we worked with received some harsh criticism from subordinates, board members and clients. It uncovered issues about her indecisiveness and lack of willingness to make tough decisions. Initially, she dismissed that feedback as simply resentment about her recent promotion, certainly a defensive reaction on her part. But when she found the courage to look more closely at the criticism, she came to recognize a pattern of behavior – dating back to early in her life – of keeping her opinions to herself, even when she had good, valid input to offer. This was a painful insight for her, as she realized that her failure to assert herself in many situations had kept her from achieving certain important objectives. Moreover, she saw she would need to experiment with new ways of acting that would feel strange and require her to take new risks.

> Usually we think that brave people have no fear. The truth is that they are intimate with fear.
>
> PEMA CHÖDRÖN

Turning and looking – exploring your past objectively and remaining committed to that process – can cause you to revisit painful emotions, such as fear, sadness, anger, or loneliness, that you thought you'd left behind. Accepting the challenge of experiencing these emotions is a giant step towards greater maturity and leadership effectiveness, but a difficult one nonetheless.

GROWING AS INDIVIDUALS AND AS LEADERS

Evidence shows that there are personal and bottom-line benefits from the process of growing up. Mature leaders make better decisions, basing them on real criteria rather than distortions caused by unconscious beliefs. Let's take a look at some critical findings.

Dr. J. Clayton Lafferty, the founder of Human Synergistics International, and the co-creator of one of our favorite leadership development tools, the Life Styles Inventory (LSI), has shown in his research that mature, self-aware leaders are more capable, more efficient, more assertive, less fearful, and have higher self-esteem. Lafferty's research demonstrates that these qualities help leaders to improve their relationships with others, enabling them to foster employee loyalty and increase productivity.

Author Jim Collins wrote a hugely popular book about business that extends Lafferty's concept, discussing qualities of the leaders of outstanding companies. In *Good to Great*, Collins' research team acquired reams of data about ten companies that had reached a certain standard of "greatness," which he defined as outstanding stock growth, evolution of brands, and success beyond their competitors.

For his book, Collins studied the leadership styles of corporate CEOs within the companies he named. All companies that achieved greatness by his measures were led by "Level Five" leaders, whom he described as self-accepting and humble, able to act calmly, showing vision, defining success through empowering others, and encouraging others to take credit. Collins further described Level Five leaders as refusing to be threatened by the successes of others, instead surrounding themselves with great people who also contributed to the companies' greatness.

Maturity goes a long way in helping leaders achieve the kind of results that Collins describes. By consciously working to overcome personal challenges, leaders learn to be more connected with people in their work. Like it or not, connections between managers and employees contribute significantly to the success of a workplace. Employees respond differently when their managers are helpful rather than frustrating to work with. Leaders in the workplace need to be respected in order to be effective, and their style of relating to others is a key element in earning respect. Those who can overcome personal insecurities can connect better with people in their work, a quality that can produce bottom-line results. It stands to reason that a leader who has worked at growing up, overcoming personal insecurities and anxieties, can relate better to people and produce exceptional results.

How do employees perceive grown-up leadership? We have spent thousands of hours with groups discussing the qualities of leaders, asking participants to match these behavioral traits with actual leaders whom they know from their own pasts. What behaviors win the confidence of workers? How do ineffective leaders discourage their team members? The responses differ slightly from group to group, but nearly always reflect the tendencies listed below.

QUALITIES OF IMMATURE LEADERS

Qualities that people identify with immature leadership include being aloof, indecisive, non-communicative, impersonal, and defensive. Immature leaders tend to blame, push people away, rely on negative reinforcement, and restrain the growth of healthy work relationships. Immature leaders tend to inflate the importance of *me* over *we*, and otherwise provide a constraint to successful achievement of goals.

Other qualities commonly identified with *immature leaders*, in no particular order, include being:

- Judgmental, patronizing, liking to play favorites, generally lacking trust in others
- Autocratic, controlling, intimidating, abusive, likely to micromanage
- Short sighted, non-collaborative
- Negative, rigid
- Dishonest, manipulative, unfair
- Unclear, avoidant
- Too busy, self-involved, likely to steal credit or pull rank
- Overemotional, indecisive, indirect, lacking in confidence

QUALITIES OF GROWN-UP LEADERS

People we've worked with describe grown-up leaders as supportive, helpful, intelligent, humanistic and team oriented. They appreciate working for bosses who demonstrate confidence in them, who share credit, and who treat people equally. These are traits and behaviors that facilitate teamwork and help employees to thrive in their workplace.

Here are more qualities commonly described as characteristic of grown-up leaders:

- Savvy, competent, resourceful, clear thinking
- Good at communicating, empathetic, flexible, creative
- Encouraging, inspiring, credit-sharing, acknowledging, compassionate, motivating
- Clear, insightful, holding high standards
- Honest, respectful, leading by example, walking the walk
- Inclined to teach and guide, offer suggestions, listen, empower

FINDING YOUR OWN STRENGTHS AND WEAKNESSES

As we said earlier, no one strives to be an immature leader. Rather than being totally effective or ineffective, most of us carry good and bad qualities in various mixtures. You may be inspiring, empathetic and warm, but lack the follow-through and decisiveness that your position requires. Or you may be bold, forceful and direct, but unable to connect with the staff in a way that inspires or empowers them to follow through.

One of our clients had practically become a bull in a china shop at work. Technically, Phil's work was brilliant. But his condescending attitude toward co-workers had become intolerable, and he was given the choice of accepting professional coaching or leaving the company. His style was seen as patronizing, rigid, intimidating and autocratic, all qualities from our "immature leaders" list. Deeply mistrustful of others, Phil resisted our initial attempts to help him. He felt like the onus should have been on his co-workers to be more accepting – and less envious – of his skills and abilities.

Management warnings to "play nice" were unsuccessful until Phil came to realize that his communication liabilities were hurting *him* more than they were hurting others. We helped him understand how he could capitalize on his strength, in this case his knowledge and expertise, if he developed better ways to share his thoughts and ideas with the world. This required him to develop maturity to recognize his weaknesses, and

---

THE EFFECTS OF PERSONAL HISTORY

Leigh Says

Growing up as the youngest kid in my family, I didn't get to make many decisions as a child. Even as an adult, my tendency is still to follow others and avoid conflict. Certainly that personal history helped me learn to become an Accommodator with my family and stay one, even into my adulthood.

HE SHE SAYS

Maureen Says

As the oldest child, and the only girl among four siblings, my opinions were often challenged while I was growing up. The best way for me to survive was to learn to defend my turf, if I ever wanted to get my needs met. In other words, I learned to become an Intimidator within my family.

---

to learn and then try using better methods for relating to others.

Knowing your strengths and weaknesses, and resolving to identify, study, and understand them, is a giant step towards personal growth. But it's a step that requires more than a superficial examination. Management requests for Phil to simply "be nicer to people" had no visible effect. The process of real and lasting growth is more complex, and takes more time and considerably more effort.

SOURCES OF FEAR

Let's consider another example: a common challenge for our coaching clients is giving negative feedback to their employees. Many leaders fear and avoid doing it. Often, clients ask us for suggestions about how to give the feedback so their employees won't become angry or emotional. We answer with a different question. We ask what the leader's experience with criticism has been – the prism through which he views giving or receiving criticism. We find that leaders who fear giving negative feedback often have experiences in their own past that makes the idea of constructive criticism frightening and uncomfortable.

As we move into discussions of assessing your skills, remember that it isn't sufficient to simply name your weaknesses and strive to become better. Rather, we ask you to probe for the *sources* of those behaviors and make a conscious effort to recognize the roles that they play in that behavior. If you are critical of yourself, take time to identify individuals from your past who were self-critical as well, or who were critical of you. What's the source of these painful images you hold?

Try to apply some of our discussion to your own situation. Look back at your answers to questions in the personal coaching session "Exploring Your Personal Prism" (pages 38–40). Did any patterns emerge that might be applicable to your life today? What insights did you notice as a result of answering the questions? The process is like trying to unravel a knot. You take one thread at a time and start a patient process of following it where it leads. Impatience makes the knot worse, as does pulling on a thread. The best possible approach is to be deliberate, unforced, and keep open to surprises and revelations.

Developing self-awareness is a challenging personal process, but one that you can take on in steps. Experience indicates that accepting the challenge is worthwhile: deep insight into personal weaknesses and challenges is a trait shared by all of the exceptional leaders that we know. We'll help you take some of those next steps in coming chapters.

DRIVING PRINCIPLES
- The process of personal change can be difficult and challenging, and requires great courage.
- Employees respond positively when their leaders are helpful, rather than frustrating, to work with.
- Knowing our own strengths and weaknesses, and working to understand them, is a giant step towards personal growth.

Your Personal Coaching Session

Examining Your Leadership Characteristics

STEP ONE

To start, write down one characteristic of yourself as a leader that you find unproductive and would like to change.

STEP TWO

Consider this characteristic in light of the prism of influences that you described in your first personal coaching session, "Examining Your Personal Prism" (pages 38–40). What clues, insights or awareness come to you regarding your characteristic as you review your answers from that exercise? Review the examples from the chart on the next page to get started.

STEP THREE

What influences do you see in your history that might contribute to the characteristic you identified? Jot down your thoughts.

STEP FOUR

List at least one personal insight that you have gained from this exercise.

Your Personal Coaching Session
(continued)

Present Unproductive Characteristics and Early Examples	Your "Prism" Categories from Chapter 2
1. Fear of hurting other's feelings *Example: You grew up constantly hearing "If you can't say something nice, don't say anything at all."*	1. Conflict; Religion; Values
2. Problems with delegation *Example: You participated in group projects in school but felt like you were often the one stuck with responsibility.*	2. Sibling Relationships; Authority; Values
3. Problems with decision making *Example: As the youngest child, you became used to having your oldest siblings make decisions for you.*	3. Authority; Conflict; Nurturing; Siblings
4. Problems dealing with angry employees *Example: Your parents' emotional outbursts were unpredictable and even scary, and you were sometimes physically hurt by them.*	4. Temperament and Emotions

Every advance, every achievement
of mankind has been connected with
an advancement in self-awareness.

CARL JUNG

CHAPTER FOUR

UNDERSTANDING
YOUR OWN TENDENCIES

If you've been doing the Personal Coaching Session exercises as you've been reading thus far, you've already taken on quite a bit of personal research in an effort to learn more about sources of your behaviors. We will now help you start to process some of that personal history and identify behavioral tendencies in an effort to connect them with your leadership capacity.

UNDERSTANDING YOUR MOTIVATION – ARE YOU AN INTIMIDATOR OR AN ACCOMMODATOR?

Why is it important to know if you are an Intimidator or Accommodator? Because most people fall into styles of habitual behavior without even thinking about it. And that's when we are least effective at accomplishing our objectives, because these habits get in the way of success.

Many leaders have a vague awareness of their struggles, but find it hard to articulate them. Those who learn to describe their challenges are also able to understand them more clearly. They become more knowledgeable about the sources of their behavior, and are in a better position to begin making changes.

Leaders who gain greater self-awareness are more likely to become growth-motivated, a concept described by Abraham Maslow as having satisfied "their basic needs for safety, belongingness, love, respect and self-esteem." The rest of us are need-motivated, and depend on our outside environment – and other people – for meeting needs. Outgrowing your need motivation will make an enormous impact on your evolution as a grown-up leader.

MOTIVATION CHARACTERISTICS

We all aspire to be growth-motivated (which is not a final destination, by the way). But to some degree, we all remain somewhat need-motivated. Accommodators, who tend to move away from others, and Intimidators, who tend to move against others, are both need-motivated. They depend too much on the outside environment to meet their needs rather than meeting needs through a healthy sense of self. As you examine characteristics of each type of person, think about their capacity as leaders.

Characteristics of
Growth-Motivated People
* Live in the moment, and put reality into a greater context
* Have a strong sense of self and others
* Are effective at interpersonal relationships
* Show high levels of creativity
* Are spontaneous, autonomous and inner-directed

Characteristics of
Need-Motivated People
* Depend on others to gratify needs
* Are easily irritated, threatened, bored by people
* Overreact to outside stimuli
* Seek the approval of others, fear failure
* Are prone to anxiety and hostility

CHARACTERISTICS OF ACCOMMODATORS AND INTIMIDATORS

If you look around you, and also at yourself, you'll quickly perceive the two clusters of tendencies that Accommodators and Intimidators tend to exhibit.

The Accommodator

- Shows an excessive need to be liked, wanted, loved, welcomed
- Values safety in the extreme
- Is highly affected by expectations and opinions of others
- Prefers to stay out of the limelight
- Tends to be policy- and procedure-driven: follows the rules first
- Secret motto: "I don't trust myself, so I will follow you."

The Intimidator

- Mistrusts others
- Assumes that the world is a jungle and that life is a contest of "survival of the fittest"
- Believes the best defense is a good offense
- Knows how to fight
- Is sometimes emotionally inhibited, uncomfortable talking about feelings
- Shows a strong need to be recognized, affirmed and praised
- Secret motto: "I don't trust you, so I will fight you to get what I need."

ACCOMMODATORS AND INTIMIDATORS

We interact with Accommodators and Intimidators daily. To help us gain insight into how their behaviors play out in the workplace, here are descriptions of two people you might meet in your job.

Both Neil and Marilyn are leaders who have achieved professional success but have hit ceilings in their effectiveness. Both are motivated and ambitious, but have realized – or have been told – that they need to acquire a greater skill set or perspective to grow as leaders. They understand that their jobs are on the line.

ACCOMMODATORS OR INTIMIDATORS?

To get some practice on identifying Accommodators and Intimidators, consider these examples.

Fictitious Accommodators you might recognize:

* Ed Norton from *The Honeymooners*
* Barney Rubble from *The Flintstones*
* Niles Crane from *Frasier*
* Gilligan from *Gilligan's Island*

Fictitious Intimidators you might recognize:

* Ralph Kramden from *The Honeymooners*
* Fred Flintstone from *The Flintstones*
* Archie Bunker from *All in the Family*
* The Skipper from *Gilligan's Island*

Can you think of other Accommodators or Intimidators from your past, whether they are real or fictitious?

MEET NEIL, THE ACCOMMODATOR

Neil: *I've been worried about my career for some time. In my last performance review, my boss, Karen, gave me feedback that suggests I'm not taking strong enough leadership of my department, and that I need to be more visible in the company.*

Neil is the leader of a product team within a large medical device organization. He has been with the company for 15 years, is highly educated, and has advanced knowledge of the products his area oversees.

Neil is warm, friendly, talkative, and receptive to others. He knows almost everyone in his workplace and is well liked, which he considers a great accomplishment. He invests a lot of time and energy in appearing kind and likeable within the organization.

Because of Neil's strong desire to be liked by all, decision making sometimes presents problems for him. He can appear indecisive, for fear of alienating someone in the process. He delays acting on important tasks until the last possible moment, creating uncertainty and anxiety for his employees and peers. His needs for approval and acceptance get in the way of his success and the success of his department.

Neil: *I have a growing sense that my clients and my employees don't value my expertise as much as I want. I want to have more influence with them and to make a bigger impact. It's frustrating, and I'm not sure how to change it.*

Lately I've been feeling like I don't really have a handle on my work team. I don't feel like we're organized or working off the same page. It gnaws at me from time to time.

It also seems like my boss doesn't have as much confidence in me as she once did. I'm afraid that I might get passed over for a promotion – or even fired – if I can't change her opinion of me.

Karen, Neil's Boss: *I've noticed that Neil's people avoid bringing issues to him for decision making for fear of creating a bottleneck – they are concerned that he will hold up the decision because he's afraid of alienating someone in the process. This is potentially a huge problem in our organization.*

I've told Neil that his inability to make decisions has led to a lack of executive presence, an area in which he needs to improve. I believe in Neil's abilities, but if he doesn't overcome this issue soon, he may have to give up his leadership position here. And that will be a loss for everyone.

MEET MARILYN, THE INTIMIDATOR

Marilyn: *I've worked hard to help build this company to where it is today. But now Bruce, my boss, is telling me that people around here are angry at me. He said that I'm too abrasive with my co-workers.*

Marilyn is CFO of a mid-size consulting business. As a "high potential leader" in her firm, she has often been considered second in command.

She has impressive skills in managing expenses and driving financial results for the firm and is considered the likely successor to Bruce, the firm's president. Bruce, however, has become increasingly uncomfortable with Marilyn's style of leadership. When the company was just getting started, Marilyn's energy and "can do" approach were real assets. Now, as CFO of a $10 million company, Marilyn manages a staff of skilled financial and accounting professionals.

Marilyn: *When Bruce started this company, he hired me to run things for him on the inside so he could concentrate on going out, networking, and finding us clients. I handled all the aspects of our operation, from finance to administration. Since I was a kid, I had always been good at handling lots of details like that – you won't find anyone who can do it better.*

I'll admit that I have high standards, but we're in a tough industry, and have grown because we provide outstanding service to our clients. I don't tolerate incompetence, and don't think there's anything wrong with that. I'm very loyal to Bruce, and I take my job very seriously. It's frustrating to me when people don't step up and do the hard work to get their jobs done around here.

If people aren't doing their job right, I have no problem telling them they have to do it differently. That's my job as a boss, isn't it? Now Bruce wants me to work with a coach. I feel totally unappreciated and like I'm being punished. As hard as I've worked for him, I can't believe that he won't stand up for me when people call me abrasive.

Bruce, Marilyn's Boss: *When I decided to start my company, I knew from the start that I wanted Marilyn to be a part of it. I knew that I could trust her to run the store. And her contributions have really helped us get where we are today.*

But as we've added people, I've noticed that Marilyn's high standards are hurting the company. Her leadership style with our staff is abrasive. It seems that the more people we have working for us, the more complaints I get about her.

Marilyn has been my right hand for years, but I'm having a real problem with her at the moment. I can't imagine running this company without her, but I'm going to lose some valuable employees if she doesn't make some changes.

In our work, we meet many people like Neil and Marilyn. In fact, it is likely that you can recognize some of their behaviors from your own work experiences. Clearly, both of them have had success using their natural leadership styles earlier in their careers. However, as the demands on their leadership abilities have grown, their tendency to revert to styles that made them successful in the past has become a liability. They have unwittingly fallen into behaviors that we often attribute to immature leaders: Neil has become indecisive, passive, and avoidant. Marilyn is rigid, abrasive, and intimidating. Both have hit ceilings in their careers and could lose their jobs as a result of their immaturity.

GAINING PERSONAL INSIGHT: A SELF-ASSESSMENT PROCESS

Neil and Marilyn demonstrate two patterns of need-based motivation: accommodating and intimidating. Neil, the Accommodator, displays more passive, approval-seeking tendencies, while Marilyn, the Intimidator, is clearly more aggressive. In our experience, most people have a natural (as well as learned) tendency to behave either like Neil or Marilyn, particularly in times of stress. Their preferences, which come from years of habit, spring from factors such as birth order, personality, gender and other life experiences.

Before we move into the next chapter, we ask you to continue to explore your own tendencies as a means of both understanding your own need-based motivation and of growing from that understanding. As we said earlier, this step of addressing anxieties and learning about weaknesses takes courage. But from our perspective, there is no more important challenge on your journey to grown-up leadership.

DRIVING PRINCIPLES

- Most people can identify with either an Accommodator or Intimidator tendency, each of which can provide significant challenges for leaders.
- Those of us who remain stuck in need-motivated behaviors are likely to hit ceilings in our effectiveness as leaders.

Your Personal Coaching Session

Assessing Your Leadership Style

Take a moment to ask yourself how you relate to the stories of Neil and Marilyn. Do you recognize your own behavior style in either of them?

Here's an exercise to assess your own tendencies. Review the list of ways people cope when under particular stress below. Circle the characteristics that fit you. At the end, you should be able to tell if you tend to be an Accommodator or an Intimidator.

STEP ONE

Please look at this list of statements and circle all that apply to you:

1. Hesitant to express opinion or be in the spotlight
2. Critical, mistrustful of others – consider others incompetent
3. Want to be liked by others
4. Prefer to stand out in a crowd

5. Often willing to put needs of others before your own needs

6. Like having the attention of others

7. Wait for others to make difficult decisions rather than being proactive

8. Prefer to be the one in charge

9. Know and follow rules carefully

10. Question the input or suggestions of others

11. Avoid confrontation

12. Able to say no to requests and ideas

13. Have doubts about your own level of competency

14. Cause confrontation

15. Tend to assume that others are more competent

16. Prefer to be alone in the limelight

17. Easier to say "yes" than "no" to others

18. Winning is a priority, despite any costs

19. Want to be included in others' projects or conversations

20. Likely to focus on minute details of a project or situation

21. Feel anxious in situations most others experience as non-threatening

22. Try to be unrealistically precise

STEP TWO

Now, tally the number of odd-numbered responses that you circled, and compare that to the number of even-numbered responses you chose. If you have more odd-numbered items, then you probably tend to be an Accommodator, while if you have more even-numbered items, you probably tend to be an Intimidator.

STEP THREE

Take a walk, sit with a cup of tea, or make time to consider this new information.

* What is your tendency: Accommodator or Intimidator?
* How does this information fit with what you know about yourself?

> ## Your Personal Coaching Session
> (continued)
>
> ● What feedback, events, conversations, or personal concerns of the last year fit with or don't match this tendency?
>
> Knowing your own tendency will be very helpful in our future discussions.
>
> ## GOING ONE STEP FARTHER
> Completing the exercise above will help you begin the important process of understanding yourself, your behaviors and your leadership tendencies. When we work with our clients, we often use assessment tools that help them gain an even greater perspective on their thinking and preferences. If you choose to do more in-depth work, we recommend two assessment tools:
>
> ### Myers Briggs Type Indicator (MBTI)
> Carl Jung's theory of psychological type was made available by Isabel Myers and Katharine Briggs through the MBTI. It is a research-tested tool and model for helping leaders understand both themselves and others. The MBTI provides a non-judgmental lens through which a leader gains a deeper understanding of how people differ in the ways they take in information, communicate, and make decisions. Insight into those differences helps a leader to value diversity in a variety of forms. It also provides tools and a greater sophistication for working with others.
>
> ### The Life Styles Inventory (LSI)
> This thinking styles assessment, developed by Clayton Lafferty, helps leaders identify their existing thinking styles and suggests specific ways to enhance their leadership effectiveness. Specifically, Lafferty's research has found that thinking styles that emphasize achievement, self-acceptance and developing supportive relationships lead to long-term success as a leader. The LSI includes both modules for self-assessment and for getting feedback from other individuals.

PART II

ACCEPTANCE AND ACTION: FOCUSING ON YOURSELF

It is not the strongest of the species that survives, nor the most intelligent, but rather the most responsive to change.

CHARLES DARWIN

CHAPTER FIVE

CONTINUING THE JOURNEY TO GROWN-UP LEADERSHIP

In the last chapter, you completed an important personal assessment exercise. You have now identified whether, in terms of your need motivation, you are more likely to act as an Accommodator or an Intimidator.

We invite you to return to that exercise for a moment now to review the statements that you circled. The circling exercise is an important step – possibly even a painful one – but it is only a start. The next step is to take this new awareness and convert it into a pathway to becoming a grown-up leader.

Before you proceed, we would like to take a moment to acknowledge the courage required to continue on this path. In our experience, we find that most leaders never examine their leadership styles in the depth that we are suggesting. The fact that you are taking this step definitely places you on "the road less traveled" and demonstrates that you are committed to your growth as a leader.

THE SKILL OF SELF-OBSERVATION

As a step in transforming awareness into enhanced leadership effectiveness, we must become tolerant, or even accepting, of the parts of ourselves that we dislike. Why is this so important?

In our experience, leaders believe in their own opinions more than in the opinions of others. But the process of change takes more than merely intellectual awareness. For real change to occur, you must *accept* what you have become aware of and make the awareness yours, at both a gut level and an intellectual level.

How do you move beyond mere intellectual awareness? The process requires desensitizing yourself to the emotional experience of observing your particular need-based style in your day-to-day behavior. The ability to take a step back and to observe your thoughts and actions from a detached perspective is a skill we call "self-observation."

> Many people who desperately hunger for power are weak. They seek power positions to compensate for their own fragility and vulnerability.
> JOHN O'DONOHUE

You will learn a great deal and gain maturity if you can get good at self-observation regarding your leadership style. Here are some important insights that can help you embrace this learning process. Think of them as self-talk, or affirmations, that you can use for support and encouragement as you proceed:

- I can observe my emotional reactions without acting on them or being held hostage by them.
- I can rationally look at situations without being overwhelmed by my emotions.

- I can learn to tolerate emotional discomfort without pushing it away.
- I can choose how I respond to activating events, rather than reacting to them out of old habit.

Deep knowledge of yourself, inextricably entwined within the awareness and acceptance process, does make you a better leader. We know that people who lead don't always feel as strong on the inside as they wish to appear on the outside. But knowing yourself well and accepting yourself, "warts and all," will give you strength.

We often coach leaders who seek control over others to compensate for self-doubt. When they gain insight into the personal fears that underlie their self-doubt, they can begin to grow in ways that are beneficial and productive within their workplaces.

> We can't connect to the world around us unless we first connect with ourselves.
>
> MELODY BEATTIE

As we have discussed, the journey through awareness and acceptance requires you to recognize the sources of your inner beliefs and demons. You also must make conscious choices about behaviors that are constructive and ones that are destructive. The journey includes the process of recognizing the work we do to appease others (as Accommodators) or control them (as Intimidators). With that insight, you can move bit by bit away from need-based motivation to the motivation that comes from your true self.

NEIL AND MARILYN RETURN

With your new insight, you are prepared now to act. In choosing possible action steps, it's appropriate to focus on both personal strengths and weakness, and to take on bite-sized tasks that keep the process manageable. In this chapter, we'll try to outline some action steps that will help to guide you through this part of the journey. But first, let's start by looking at the personal processes of Neil and Marilyn, the leaders we met in Chapter 3, and by considering how they move through the Awareness-Acceptance-Action (AAA) model for change (see page 19).

NEIL'S PROCESS

Let's look at how the Awareness-Acceptance-Action process evolved for Neil.

Neil: *It has been really hard for me to go through this process. The key thing I notice is how difficult it is for me to keep from putting too much weight on other people's opinions. I'm noticing it more and more when I get a critical look from my boss, or a client, or even when my wife disagrees with me. I notice how easily I'm tempted to give in to them and do what I think they want.*

As he analyzed his personal prism, Neil developed a self-portrait that gave him new insights. As a young child, Neil was encouraged to develop a great sense of consideration and caring for others. As a consequence, he did not cultivate a clear awareness of his own opinions and desires. This served Neil well in his family, who greatly valued consideration of others. However, it was causing him to become indecisive as

---

STAR TREK ON LEADERSHIP

In "The Enemy Within," an episode from the original *Star Trek* TV series, Captain James T. Kirk gets mysteriously changed as he is beamed up to the *U.S.S. Enterprise.* A transporter malfunction splits him into the "good and honorable" Kirk and the "evil" Kirk who runs amok on his ship. "Good" Kirk is vulnerable, having lost his ability to make important decisions. "Bad" Kirk does some violent things, but it becomes clear that there are elements in this half of his moral fiber that contribute to Kirk's overall qualities as an effective leader. Ultimately, we see that neither Kirk can survive without his other half: both sides play vital roles in his capacity as a qualified starship captain.

The episode reminds us of one of our favorite Pema Chödrön quotes: "Our neuroses and our wisdom are made out of the same material. If you throw out your neurosis, you also throw out your wisdom." Who said you can't learn anything by watching TV?

---

a leader. He also recognized that this indecisiveness regularly kept him from achieving his desired workplace outcomes.

Then, after receiving feedback from colleagues and thinking about his leadership style, Neil became more aware of how his behavior impact-ed others at work. Over time, as he turned and looked, he learned more about his beliefs, and could understand how they were actually affecting his workplace. The awareness that relationships from his past constrained his development as a leader was initially horrifying to Neil, but over time he was able to recognize and own his actions, and accept his accommodating nature as an area he must address.

> Speak your mind, even
> if your voice shakes.
> UNKNOWN

Neil's job continued to present everyday struggles. He needed to get better at recognizing and expressing his own ideas, negotiating based on his assessment of a situation, and recognizing that his colleagues and team members at work really wanted him to be himself.

Neil: *It's so frustrating to try to change. But I am learning to trust my-self a little more. I've tried to catch myself when I start to feel defen-sive – to think before I respond, and to be less hard on myself.*

How do I respond differently? I was in a meeting the other day and something I did was criticized. But instead of getting quiet like I usu-ally do, I asked a question to clarify what people meant, and listened closely to the answers. The input was really quite helpful, I noticed.

I'm learning to listen to myself more, not to give other people's opin-ions quite so much weight. I have always assumed that others were right, but now I'm trying to think of their ideas as input, or data, but not as the truth. This helps me listen to myself more.

I'm realizing that I can have more confidence in myself – that's how I can do a better job. I know a lot about my work, and my colleagues believe that, too. My job is to set direction for my team, and I don't necessarily have to have everyone's agreement before I act. It slows us down and is frustrating to everyone.

My boss says I'm a good strategic thinker and values my ideas. I'm working on trusting that and acting on it more often.

Neil started to think about the present-day consequences of saying what he thought, and the courage that speaking up would require. He wanted to learn that as a leader he could survive disapproval.

As Neil continued a daily self-reflection for several weeks, he noticed a quiet yet powerful determination within himself to get better in his job. From day to day, he could own his actions without the emotional hook that snagged him when he began the process. Shedding baggage, he became ready to examine ways in which he could act differently in his work.

Marilyn's process

What does Marilyn's journey through awareness and acceptance look like, and how can she now convert that determination into action? What are some changes that she might consider making so she can deal with and eventually overcome her hostile tendencies?

Marilyn: *I was mortified when I saw the results of my personal assessment. I had no idea that people saw me as mean, angry, and intolerant. It was never my intention to hurt people. I'm blown away by these results.*

I'm hearing feedback that I typically talk as if I'm ready for a fight, and that I often act as if I have armor on, as if I need to protect myself.

My coach is trying to help me figure out where this behavior came from. I grew up in a big family, where I was the oldest kid and the only girl, with four younger brothers. Someone was always bickering in my house, which I thought was normal for all families. But I'm starting to realize that we had more arguments than normal, and as the only girl, I was in the middle of lots of them. I guess I really did need to protect myself.

One way I survived was by doing well in whatever I did. I set high standards for myself. They still come in handy at work, and have really helped the company grow. But I'm starting to learn how they hurt me and others as well – by adding stress to my life while often demeaning my staff. It's frustrating when my people don't get the job done the right way, but I guess it's hard when my high standards are in place for everyone all the time. I think that's where my abrasiveness comes from.

I do care about the people I work with, and believe that they're competent. I'm starting to see that my inclination to argue or protect myself can stifle others and keep them from coming to me. I really don't want them to feel that way. I'm actively working to change my knee-jerk reactions using a four-step process I learned from my coach: literally sit on my hands, count to ten, take a deep breath, and listen.

Clearly, Marilyn's high-stress reaction to work was wearing her down. She was over-working, over-doing, and over-compensating. In the midst of her struggles, she literally didn't see any other alternatives to her behavior until she took time to turn and look, become aware, and start to accept her needs so she could move beyond them.

At work, Marilyn gained insight into the armor that she carried with her in life. It became a barrier that insulated her from people around her. She frequently disengaged from others, while remaining constantly aware of the tasks she needed to perform in order to maintain that armor. She began to recognize feelings of being out of control that caused her to dig in her feet, becoming stubborn and belligerent. She paid more attention to how she reacted when she feared her armor wasn't protecting her well.

Deep down, Marilyn wanted to motivate and encourage her people to set high standards. How ironic, then, was it when she heard her workers report that they wished they could see her "human" side. Her armor was literally yielding the opposite results that she desired, practically weighing her down with the problems of her entire department.

DIFFERENT ACTIONS NEEDED

Action steps will look different for each individual. Neil, the Accommodator, wants to be seen by his peers as competent and insightful. But he needs to find his courage and his "voice," to be truly present at work. He will be more effective when he starts to share his opinions and ideas more often and more forcefully.

Conversely Marilyn, the Intimidator, needs to learn to let down her guard and to back down from confrontations. She uses her opinions aggressively and doesn't make room for other ideas. By insulating herself, she fails to listen. That practice discourages people she works with from being truly engaged.

For leaders like Marilyn and Neil, journeys through awareness, acceptance and action will help them to become more effective and productive leaders. The extremity of their natural tendencies will evolve into a more productive pattern of behavior. They will be better able to step out of their personal fears and anxieties, and will learn to deal with situations without the baggage of their outmoded habits.

> The main difference between effective and ineffective leaders at the top of organizations is the degree of interpersonal sensitivity displayed by the leader.
> MORGAN McCALL

The first quality of grown-up leadership: maturity

As you move through the AAA process, you gain insight into your more extreme tendencies and begin to take actions to moderate them. Hopefully, a new era begins, one in which you become more comfortable in your own skin and feel like you belong at the grown-up table. This middle area represents growth for both Intimidators and Accommodators alike, a place where you can connect better with people, and be more honest, respectful, and authentic.

While the actions you might need to take to reach this new, higher stage of maturity will be particular to your own personality and issues, maturity is *the* ultimate goal that we all can strive to achieve. And as we've seen repeatedly, maturity is vital to becoming a great leader.

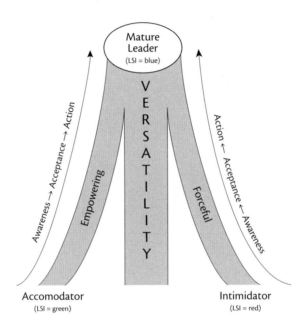

GAINING MATURITY AS A LEADER

Mature Leader
(LSI = blue)

V E R S A T I L I T Y

Awareness → Acceptance → Action

Empowering

Action ← Acceptance ← Awareness

Forceful

Accomodator
(LSI = green)

Intimidator
(LSI = red)

Each of us tends to naturally favor one of two styles of leadership – empowering or forceful. For teaching purposes, we identify leaders who fall into the extremes of these styles as Accomodators and Intimidators. (In terms of Life Styles Inventory types, they are green and red, respectively. See page 59.)

If you lead using only your natural style, you will not be as effective as you can be in all situations. Thus it pays to use the Awareness-Acceptance-Action process to identify your natural style, understand and accept it, and then learn to use the complementary style when situations call for it.

When you can consciously choose an appropriate style of leadership, you'll find yourself becoming a truly mature leader (in LSI terms, a blue type).

TAKING ACTION: WHAT IT LOOKS LIKE

How can Accommodators Grow Towards Maturity?

How can Intimidators Grow Towards Maturity?

Accommodators Need to Practice:
- Accepting responsibility
- Taking on challenging tasks
- Trusting in their own ideas
- Learning how to motivate others
- Speaking up more often, with conviction

Intimidators Need to Practice:
- Sharing responsibility
- Learning to accept change
- Involving others in decisions
- Being more cooperative, encouraging, and friendly
- Avoiding defensive behaviors

Action steps:
- Pick one new idea or opinion and commit yourself to expressing it and following it through to completion.
- Confront an employee who isn't performing well.
- Make time to hear your inner voice. Write at least one page in a journal, three to four times a week, to see what you have to say about life.
- Propose a new initiative to motivate your team.
- Share an idea, plan, or explore a perplexing question or challenge with a colleague to develop more trust.

Action steps:
- Take some time to get to know the people you work with better.
- Take 10 to 15 minutes a day to walk around your office and check in with your team. Find out about their lives, their families, and listen to them as they tell you what they're working on.
- Next time your are in a conflict, focus on your own behavior instead of that of the other person. Try to identify how you are contributing to the conflict, and modify your action as needed.
- Seek out opportunities to build individual relationships. Say "I care about you. How can I help?"

DEFINING ACCEPTANCE

HE SHE SAYS

Leigh Says

For an Accommodator – a person who is compliant, avoids confrontation, and is a peacekeeper – acceptance requires you to gather up your inner determination to make changes. These changes will certainly take courage. But if you use this process to gather your personal strength, you can turn outward and focus on becoming more visible in the space around you. Turning outward will help you improve in your role as leader.

Maureen Says

For those among us who are Intimidators, who relish bickering and even pick an occasional fight, we need to turn and look, then use the acceptance process to learn and practice surrender. We can overcome our challenges by learning to back off, let go of situations, and take things less personally. By turning inward, we gain skills that will help us behave differently at times, and that can make us better leaders.

In coming chapters, we'll help you identify skills that will be helpful in taking these action steps. But keep up with us, because we have more qualities of exceptional leadership to discuss.

DRIVING PRINCIPLES

- As an observer of your own behavior, you can gain perspective on your strengths, and become less fearful of your weaknesses.
- The Awareness-Acceptance-Action model can help you understand the process of personal change and move towards maturity.
- Taking action requires more than thinking – it requires the energy to try new behaviors.
- Grown-up leaders are better able to overcome their fears and anxieties when responding to workplace challenges.

Your Personal Coaching Session

Developing Your Plan for Awareness-Acceptance-Action

The goal of this growth exercise is to increase your awareness and acceptance of your current thinking and behavior, and to increase your determination to make changes if you so choose. This is best accomplished as part of a gradual, ongoing process that takes place regularly over the coming weeks. You will find that successfully working through introspective and goal-setting exercises such as this can dramatically help you move towards greater maturity as a leader.

Weeks 1 and 2: Your daily awareness and acceptance log

Set aside at least 15 minutes a day for the next two weeks. (Put a daily reminder into your PDA or calendar.) Some prefer to make time just after they wake up or before they go to sleep, while others prefer to block out the beginning or end of their work-day. What's important is to make time available daily for personal reflection. We recommend devoting a separate notebook to this project.

Having gone through the self-assessment exercise in Chapter 3, and having determined whether your personal behavior style is skewed either towards the Accommodator or the Intimidator, write the answers to the following four questions into your notebook each day:

- What personal actions or behaviors did I notice in the past day that demonstrate my tendencies toward an accommodating or intimidating style?
- What was I thinking, remembering, or feeling when those situations arose?
- What impact did these thoughts or feelings make on that situation?
- How did my actions in those situations affect the outcome I wanted?

Week 3: Creating a personal action plan

At the start of your third week, complete the following statements to set one or two personal development goals based on your insights. Try to avoid the tendency to overdo it – one goal at a time is sufficient for most of us.

Your Personal Coaching Session

- The specific goal I would like to set for myself is: (Describe it as specifically as possible.)
- A realistic timeline for completion of this goal is:
- I will complete this goal by:
- The behavior I want to modify (or what I want to do differently) is:
- People who already behave as I'd like to include: (Can you talk with them or observe them?)
- I will practice this new behavior on or with: (List names. Practice is important in lasting change. Let them know what you are doing, and ask for feedback if you are comfortable doing so.)
- The books or courses that will help me learn more about the new behavior I am trying to achieve include: (You may have to set a sub-goal to research this.)
- I will be successful when:
- The difference others will notice is:

Weeks 4 through 6

Depending on what goals you've set and how often you get a chance to practice your changes, you should set check-points to monitor your progress and even "grade" your success. The point is to weave this practice into your life rather than view it as a single event. And needless to say, once you've reached one goal, you're welcome to start work on the next!

When all you have is a hammer,
everything tends to look
like a nail.

ABRAHAM MASLOW

CHAPTER SIX

LEADERSHIP VERSATILITY: BUILDING A BIGGER TOOLBOX

Grown-up leaders expand beyond their natural skills in order to achieve exceptional success. Motivating, coaching and developing others requires you to make a clear commitment to learning new skills. As we have discussed, your personal development is a key step. In this chapter, we examine another quality of grown-up leadership: versatility.

A WIDER RANGE OF SKILLS

Imagine a home-repair specialist who arrives at your home to tackle a number of tasks that have been begging for attention. He is highly qualified and knows a lot about all parts of your home. Suppose, however, that he arrives with only a small toolbox containing the most basic of tools: a hammer, screwdriver, saw, and pliers. No matter how good he is, and no matter how good the quality of his four tools, he's going to have trouble making some of the repairs you need.

To keep your home in good repair, you need a full tool kit to handle the variety of jobs that you face. Likewise, those who lead others need to have a wide range of appropriate, effective tools in their leadership toolboxes. Because even if you own the best hammer on the market, you won't be able to fix or improve something that requires a monkey wrench.

The second quality of grown-up leadership: versatility

To be well equipped to lead in a grown-up way, you need to be adept at using a variety of interaction styles and skills. (Please take a moment now to review the model on page 68.) For most people, one style of relating to others comes most naturally, feels the most comfortable, and gives them the greatest confidence. But growing up as a leader requires adding complementary skills. This process of gaining *versatility* can at first feel unnatural and quite difficult. But you will need these new tools if you want to be able to reach a higher level of leadership success.

Examples of versatility are all around us. Great actors need a variety of skills to effectively portray a range of characters and avoid type casting. Great golfers need more than a long, straight drive: they must also be adept at approach shots, chipping and putting. A great cook understands how to use more seasonings than simply salt and pepper and to be sensitive to the level of seasoning to use. A great teacher needs to be clear, inspiring, challenging, supportive – and sometimes, needs to maintain order!

All leaders have preferred styles. As we discussed in Chapter 2, your preferred style evolves from both your natural, inborn temperament and your personal history. These experiences are part of your fiber and constitution, and an extension of the personal belief systems that you examined in earlier Personal Coaching Session exercises.

Let's take another look at Albert Ellis' Structure of Interpretation to understand the importance of versatility. (Here's a quick refresher on Ellis' theory: (A) Activating Events are filtered through (B) our personal belief systems before we respond with (C) consequential thoughts, emotions and behavior. See page 34 to review the model.)

By now you have developed a better understanding of your own beliefs, your personal prism through which you see the world. Having become more aware of that prism, you have gotten better at recognizing how it affects you in your work and personal life. Hopefully, you have accepted that your own style isn't inherently good or bad, but simply a reality for you.

Just as you have a natural personal style, you have a natural leadership style as well. We notice that most Accommodators tend to prefer an empowering style, while most Intimidators are more comfortable using a forceful leadership approach. Both empowering and forceful leadership styles have numerous positive qualities, but both have potential drawbacks as well. Let's reexamine our list of characteristics of mature and immature leaders to see how forceful and empowering styles can be used in both mature and immature ways:

MATURE LEADERSHIP CHARACTERISTICS	IMMATURE LEADERSHIP CHARACTERISTICS
Empowering	**Empowering**
Good communicator	Indecisive
Empathic	Overly emotional
Encouraging, shares credit	Self-doubting
Compassionate	Unclear, avoids confrontation
Forceful	**Forceful**
Motivating	Autocratic
Holds up high standards	Too busy
Leads by example	Rigid
Decisive	Controlling

If you think about leaders you have admired, you'll notice that most mature leaders use both leadership styles – empowering *and* forceful – depending on the situation. They're the ones who have learned versatility. They've expanded their toolboxes by adding skills that complement their natural ones.

LEADERSHIP STYLES IN ACTION: NEIL AND MARILYN

Let's check back in on Neil and Marilyn. Through them, we can illustrate how the positive and negative characteristics inherent in empowering and forceful styles play out. Accommodators like Neil often use a natural empowering leadership style, and Intimidators like Marilyn typically use a natural forceful style. Both run into problems, however, when they only use their preferred styles. Their inability to develop the complementary style causes them problems we commonly see in many leaders we coach. In short, they each need to add more tools to their toolboxes.

Neil and Marilyn have been working for six months now on their leadership skills. The deficiencies in Neil and Marilyn's leadership abilities are now clearer to them, and they have begun to make dramatic changes by working through the AAA process. By focusing on learning versatility, they are taking huge steps forward in their work and personal lives. Their bosses and colleagues have noticed as well.

NEIL AND MARILYN MAKE PROGRESS

Neil: *Work has been going much better for me. Recently I had an idea about how to support our products in the marketplace, and that process is starting to catch on throughout the organization and make a difference for our clients. I also added a new way to measure client satisfaction that we never used before.*

I'm feeling much better about managing people. I have had individual meetings with all seven employees who report to me, and have committed to meeting with them monthly. All of them have set specific performance objectives, and I'm trying to give them all positive and negative feedback to help them reach those goals. Our team feels more cohesive to me – like we're moving in a good direction together.

Last week I got an e-mail from my boss that said she's noticed how I'm taking more charge in my department, and that the change seems to be making a big difference around here. That hasn't happened before. I felt like she was speaking as my partner rather than my boss.

It's still hard for me to trust myself and speak up – I've kept my ideas pent up in so many meetings that it's difficult to change suddenly. I'm taking some time before meetings to consider my objectives and think about how I can make them happen. That's become a very helpful process for me. I'm also spending time by myself every morning before I start work, and that helps me a lot.

Karen, Neil's Boss: *Neil has made great progress recently. He seems to be much more in charge of his work area. I have more confidence that Neil adds value to the company. I've felt much more comfortable inviting him into meetings with my peers and am feeling good about the input he offers.*

I've always liked what he has to say, but now I notice that I like HOW he's saying it. He seems much less hesitant, doesn't back down as easily, and is much less passive in meetings. His ideas are good, and he's standing up for them, which gives them more impact.

I have especially noticed how he interacts with his staff lately. He's providing more direction, and they're really responding well. They seem happier, and are performing at a higher level than before.

Neil still backs down more quickly than I'd like, and he still hesitates to talk in meetings with senior management. I wish he'd make better eye contact and speak louder and more firmly in those meetings – it would help him demonstrate his confidence in his ideas. I'm trying to show him that by being more forceful, he'll make a stronger impression.

Marilyn: *I can't believe how tightly wound I was. I feel much more at peace these days at work. I've worked with my coach on learning how to recharge my batteries and reduce the stress in my life.*

When I first started working with my coach, she said I needed to find some way outside of work to spend time alone doing something I enjoyed. I started reading for pleasure every night before I go to bed. I had forgotten that I like to read, and it seems to have made a lot of difference.

Life at work and at home seems more relaxed. I have a teenage daughter, and I hadn't realized how much I was pushing her. Now I'm trying to have more fun with her, rather than always drilling her for information, and we both are thoroughly enjoying that.

Last month, something funny happened at work, and I made a joke about it and laughed out loud. Bruce, my boss, told me he hadn't heard me laugh in years. I forgot that I have a sense of humor, and have started taking the risk of letting it out more often. It seems to soften people up and make the days less stressful.

Bruce, Marilyn's Boss: *I'm amazed at the changes I've seen in Marilyn. She really seems to understand how her abrasiveness has hurt others, and she is making some big adjustments. I've noticed that she sometimes catches herself and changes her actions midstream. I'm just not getting many complaints about her these days. It's a huge relief.*

People don't seem as hesitant about approaching her. She takes time to visit THEM, something she never did before. She's meeting with people, going to lunch with them, smiling, and laughing. I hadn't seen her laugh in years. Suddenly everyone's noticed that she has a sense of humor. She's really funny, and it's great to hear her laugh.

The effect around here has been amazing. The office seems like a happier place. People don't seem as burned out, particularly Marilyn. One of our employees told me Marilyn worked with him to set some new goals for his work, and that her standards seemed much more reasonable.

Don't get me wrong – we had a huge deadline last week, and Marilyn really got her team motivated to get the proposal out on time. They did a great job, too. It's good to know that she can still pull out all the stops when she needs to.

When we first met Neil and Marilyn, we could detect fears or reluctance about adopting behavior from the complementary style. Neil, an Accommodator, resisted the idea of trying to be more forceful. Marilyn hadn't considered learning empowering tools before – as an Intimidator, she was so ready for fights that she never thought about the effect her style had on others.

> Managers who emphasize one [leadership style] to the point of sacrificing the other put themselves and their organizations at risk.
>
> ROBERT KAPLAN

One reason that versatility remains so elusive is that people feel prejudiced against the style they lack, as we've clearly seen in Neil and Marilyn. But empowering and forceful styles don't have to be viewed as opposed styles – they are really complementary. By being more open-minded, Neil and Marilyn are becoming more grown-up leaders by developing the complementary skills and becoming truly versatile.

ACKNOWLEDGING YOUR BELIEF SYSTEM

Why do you think people are biased against the leadership style that complements their own natural one? Let's return to Ellis' ABC model. Buried somewhere deep inside your personal beliefs lie some biases about how good leaders should act. These beliefs are frequently based in early childhood experiences you had with a given authority figure, one who demonstrated an *immature* version of either the empowering or forceful style. As a reaction against the unpleasant effects of that behavior, you try to avoid inflicting that same discomfort on the people you currently lead.

For example, you might have had a particularly forceful piano teacher in your early years who made it difficult to learn, unpleasant to come to lessons, and downright frustrating for you as a young student. Your memories of the immature forcefulness of that teacher may still be causing you, as an adult, to avoid using a forceful style with your workers. Your empowering style probably has suited you well for many years and carried you through many situations.

But looking at it objectively, you would grant that forceful leaders bring many effective qualities to their work. To avoid being forceful at *all* times simply limits your leadership scope. That suggests your biases against forcefulness are more emotional than rational. They are born out of fears based on that bad example of a forceful style, years ago.

But there are many mature ways to use forceful or empowering styles. Forceful behavior can be a great motivator of people when high performance is crucial or a deadline is imminent. Conversely, an empowering approach can help employees gain confidence or take more ownership of an idea or process.

We have seen organizations act upon biases against a past leader's style, too, by overvaluing a particular skill set when they hire a new leader, hoping to compensate for the predecessor's weakness. For example, a company replacing a leader with a particularly forceful style may unconsciously – or consciously – seek a candidate with an enabling style, a person with a reputation for employee involvement, because that quality was missing under the previous leader.

So a new person is hired for that role, thanks to her reputation as an empowering leader. But one year into the job, her approach is not successful, perhaps due to past expectations, workplace culture, or market considerations. If she only knows how to use her empowering style, then she will most likely fail to achieve her objectives whenever a more forceful approach is needed. If she had cultivated her capacity to use the complementary forceful style, she would have been more likely to succeed as a leader.

The point is clear: leaders cannot become truly mature unless they can pivot in either direction – toward empowering leadership or toward forceful leadership – as a situation warrants. But if they have not sufficiently examined the baggage inherent in their own collection of beliefs and experiences, then they will be trapped by biases, and will not become adequately versatile.

LEARNING AND PRACTICING VERSATILITY

Versatility doesn't require you to change your dominant tendency in leading. In fact, your ability to learn complementary skills will help give your natural skills greater impact.

Think of a soprano opera singer with a breathtakingly high voice. If she is to become a star, she also needs to expand her range, learn how to adjust her volume, and use subtle nuances to express the meaning of the music she sings. If the high range voice is all she uses, she will wear it out. By learning vocal techniques that help her hit a variety of notes and volume levels, her high notes will have more impact on audiences.

> In life, it's not so much where you have been that counts. It's what you have learned from where you have been that has meaning.
>
> UNKNOWN

Likewise, naturally empowering leaders who can be forceful when necessary may find that their empowering style works more effectively because they use it less often. And practically speaking, a versatile leader (like a well-trained soprano) will get more roles to play.

Ultimately, the greatest barrier to versatility is self-doubt. If you are overly attached to either forceful or empowering characteristics, those beliefs will get in the way of your success. Overcoming self-doubt and eliminating your bias against complementary styles will help you develop a more grown-up leadership style.

You will need courage to try out and perfect new skills, especially ones that feel very unfamiliar. But with practice, you can learn to back off in some situations, to be more prying or forceful in others, and most important, to recognize the signs that something different from your natural style is called for. We will help you examine these tools in the upcoming chapters.

DRIVING PRINCIPLES

- You can learn skills that will complement your natural leadership style.
- Different workplace challenges require an ability to adapt your leadership styles to the demands of each situation.
- Exceptional leaders know how and when to be forceful and when to be empowering.

Your Personal Coaching Session

Expanding Your Leadership Versatility

By now, you are familiar with our philosophy: Becoming a grown-up leader takes a regular, sustained, even daily approach to gaining personal insight and trying new behaviors. We suggest completing the following exercise as a way to assess your own leadership versatility, and as a means of expanding your tool box.

Step One

Take a few moments to answer the following questions, and to set some specific goals for yourself to help you develop more versatility in your leadership style. Use bullet points, statements, paragraphs or individual words to respond, whichever feels most comfortable to you.

- What is your preferred leadership style: empowering or forceful?
- Do you understand a connection between that style and your tendencies towards intimidating or accommodating behaviors?
- How do you feel about the style that complements your preferred one?
- How versatile are you today (low, medium, high)?
- What do you base your answer on?
- What level of versatility does your job require?
- What level would you like to have?

Your Personal Coaching Session
(continued)

Step Two

Now, think of an example of a current work situation where you might practice more of your complementary style. Answer the following questions based on that situation:

- How could you act differently in this situation, using the complement to your natural style?
- What specific actions can you take to become more comfortable with the style you will need?
- When can you complete these actions?
- Given these steps, how do you plan to approach this situation, and what will be your objectives for the outcome?
- How will you know you made progress?

You can employ men and women
to work for you, but you must win their hearts
to have them work with you.

TIORIO

CHAPTER SEVEN

ENGAGING OTHERS THROUGH RELATIONSHIP-BASED LEADERSHIP

There are many benefits to learning about your own need-based motivations, and to gaining greater understanding of your style as either an Accommodator or an Intimidator. So far, we have discussed in depth how gaining greater insight into yourself can help you to mature, add skills, and make steady, conscious changes in your behavior.

But there's another major benefit: the lessons you are learning can be applied to your relationships with others as well. As a leader, these lessons will help you gain a better understanding about the people you lead. It is valuable to know and become more aware of your own style, but it is equally valuable to understand where your employees are coming from and what motivates them.

In this chapter we will discuss a concept we call relationship-based leadership, which we define as leading others in a way that links an employee's purpose, talents, values and interests to organizational objectives. Relationship-based leadership, which some call employee engagement or talent management, is more than a nice way to keep people satisfied in their job. It's a company's ethical and business imperative that enhances productivity and affects the bottom line.

Relationship-based leadership is most effective when practiced by grown-up leaders who can relate to their workers while remaining involved, yet objective; connected, yet detached; focused, yet adaptable. Leaders who recognize the Accommodators and the Intimidators on their teams fundamentally understand the different strengths and weaknesses each brings to their work, and tailor strategies to engage and motivate them in appropriate ways. Such leaders ultimately encourage a more productive workforce.

The third quality of grown-up leadership: relationship-based leadership

Sometime in the last generation, most companies changed the name of the personnel departments within their organizations, opting for the term more commonly used today, human resources. This was no euphemistic change engineered to help make workplaces more politically correct. Rather, it was recognition of the complexity of the task of managing people and the fact that people are among the most precious resources any organization taps.

The change in terminology effectively recognized that people have minds, wills, likes, dislikes, strengths, and weaknesses. In making the switch, industry affirmed that managing people required a more relational perspective. People were no longer being seen as herds of cattle who could be prodded and moved at will, but workers who needed – and responded to – a more personal approach.

The term *human resources* implies that employees have needs, and that companies set out to recognize and address those needs as they pertain to the objectives of the company. Employees are human beings who are put on the earth with an inherent need for meaning and purpose. Work that utilizes their talents, skills and interests productively can be a source of that purpose. It's the relationship between the manager and the employee that fosters the linkage between company objectives and employee development. That's your job as a leader.

We have always fundamentally believed in this linkage between employee engagement and organizational success. We emphasize to the leaders we work with that, by growing beyond competency with tasks, they build strong relationships with those around them to achieve big picture objectives. This relational style, when balanced with maturity, determination and versatility, will help you successfully engage and motivate employees at all levels.

What does an engaged employee look like, you ask? Leaders we work with say that engaged employees:

- Are clear about the purpose of their work.
- Seek better ways to do their jobs.
- Work with a high level of energy, a high need for achievement.
- Are upbeat and proud to work for the organization.
- Feel committed to positive team results.
- Bring their full selves (i.e., brains and passions) to work regularly.

Do you want a company full of employees with these traits? Evidence suggests you should, if you want to achieve your business objectives. The link between engagement and productivity has grown well beyond a hypothesis. In recent years, solid evidence has emerged that helps define the link between employee development and business outcomes. For example, one extensive research study, conducted by the Gallup Organization, created a way to measure the elements necessary to "attract, focus and keep the most talented employees." In another, a real-life example, executives from Sears, Roebuck and Company rebuilt the company's corporate culture and measures for success around one core tenet: employee attitude.

We find the Gallup study, examined in depth in *First, Break all the Rules* (*FBAR*) by Marcus Buckingham and Curt Coffman, particularly useful because it moves far beyond many of the generalizations present in business today. Rather than simply concluding that engaged employees are more likely to remain in a job longer, their findings concluded that "turnover is mostly a management issue. If you have a turnover problem, look first to your manager." To us, that sounds like a problem that requires relationship-based leadership as a solution.

In its company's efforts to build sales and profits, Sears' executives in-

---

THE SEARS QUESTIONS: EMPLOYEES' ATTITUDES ABOUT THEIR JOBS AND THE COMPANY

Leaders at Sears, Roebuck and Company developed these questions to measure the attitudes of their employees. Sears found that positive responses to these ten questions had a positive impact on the company's bottom line.

- Do you like the kind of work you do?
- Does your work give you a sense of accomplishment?
- How do you feel about working at Sears?
- How does the amount of work you are expected to do influence your overall attitude about your job?
- How do your physical working conditions influence your overall attitude about your job?
- How does the way you are treated by those who supervise you influence your overall attitude about your job?
- How do you feel about the future of the company?
- Is Sears is making the changes necessary to compete effectively?
- Do you understand our business strategy?
- Do you see a connection between the work you do and the company's strategic objectives?

Source: Harvard Business Review

---

vested many hours "listening to customers and employees, studying best practices at other companies, thinking about what would constitute world-class performance at Sears, and establishing measures and objectives." From that data, a group of 150 senior-level managers, known as The Phoenix Team, gradually developed a formula for the company's success that would both increase customer satisfaction and raise revenue. This formula was built on the same foundation that the *FBAR* authors found: employee attitude.

> If your relationship with your manager is fractured, then no amount of in-chair massaging or company-sponsored dog walking will persuade you to stay and perform. It is better to work for a great manager in an old-fashioned company than for a terrible manager in a company offering an enlightened, employee-focused culture.
>
> Marcus Buckingham and Curt Coffman

In short, both Sears and *FBAR* recognized that employee *attitudes* about their job and about the company had a direct impact on employee *behavior*, which in turn had bottom-line impacts for companies. Sears even went one step farther, identifying a new set of criteria upon which they would evaluate their corporate leaders. These included interpersonal skills, empowerment skills, communications skills, integrity, and employee development. In other words, they embraced relationship-based leadership.

So now we have evidence. Companies find that they have more productive employees, less turnover, and a more positive work environment if they strive for employee engagement. Unfortunately, the management model we often see is not relational at all: Managers send employees off to work on their tasks. The employees report to their managers (infrequently) on how they are doing on those tasks, and they get a performance review once a year, full of feedback about their task accomplishment.

Growing up as a leader includes learning to be collaborative, relational, and versatile. Based on these two examples, it's clear that today's fast-changing business environment demands that leaders become as expert at people management as they are about their products and services. If we recognize the importance of engaging employees in achieving bottom-line results, then we must also recognize that engaging them is the responsibility of those who lead.

DEVELOPING A RELATIONSHIP-BASED APPROACH

Mature leaders recognize that the process of engaging people in their work requires ongoing efforts to build authentic relationships. But this requires more than lip service. For example, simply giving out "kudos" at staff meetings might meet some employees' needs for recognition, but may backfire if the praise is seen as undeserved, insincere, or simply meant to motivate. Instead, leaders need to incorporate relationship-based leadership principles into all facets of their approach, working on ways to clarify expectations, encourage growth, build teams, value opinions, and enhance collaboration.

Our own research indicates that certain behaviors help leaders engage employees and improve their productivity. Practicing these behaviors and making them become habits will help you create an environment in which employees feel engaged. Do you want to grow as a relationship-based leader? Here are some suggestions you can use to cultivate stronger connections with people you lead:

- Demonstrate that employees' work makes a difference, and that they are noticed.
- Notice how employees are developing in their work, and actively encourage further growth.
- Make an effort to get to know team members as individuals.
- Share insights that help employees understand their own talents and capabilities.
- Define expectations in a way that increases clarity of tasks and responsibilities.
- Demonstrate that you seek out and take employees' opinions seriously.

Too often, leaders view interacting with employees as a bother or as one more interruption of the leader's real work of completing his or her own tasks. We believe this thinking is fundamentally wrong. To be a grown-up leader, you must recognize that a passion for working with and developing your employees is at the very heart of your success. Remember, you achieve results through others. Therefore, your job must include tasks such as:

- Aligning your staff around a common direction.
- Working with your people to set challenging, meaningful goals.
- Providing frequent and meaningful feedback.
- Understanding your employees' talents and aspirations.
- Helping to link those talents to company objectives.

If you do not want to do these things, you do not want to lead.

However, if you *do* want to be a grown-up leader, you need to focus on actions that will positively affect the attitudes of employees. Research indicates that you will be rewarded with greater loyalty, productivity and achievement of objectives. To set the stage and create an environment to really engage people, try some of these concrete suggestions in your office:

- Encourage employees to become involved in projects that stretch their skills, providing coaching and guidance so they succeed.
- Show an interest in details about employees' lives, remembering key information and following up.
- Give appropriate praise or credit when deserved, in front of others when possible.
- Provide an unexpected reward to recognize hard work completed or times of stress.
- Invite staff to participate in meetings, teams or task forces that might expand their horizons.

DRIVING PRINCIPLES

- Evidence shows that employees' connections with their direct supervisors have profound impacts on their loyalty and ultimate workplace performance.
- We can maximize the output and efforts of our team by cultivating relationships with the people we lead.
- As leaders, we need to become as expert in people management as we are in our own fields of work.

Your Personal Coaching Session

Engaging an Employee

Step One

Schedule a coffee or lunch appointment with a valued employee on the subject of employee engagement. In this process, we encourage you to share some of your own experiences (neither advice nor expectations) as well. Below is a list of questions that will help you start a dialogue.

- What are the three to five most important talents you bring to your job?
- What talents are most important for success in your job?
- What projects or tasks are the most satisfying for you at work?
- What engages you most at work?
- What accomplishments in the last year are you most proud of?
- What are you interested in learning more about?
- At work, things are easiest when:
- At work, things are hardest when:

Step Two

After the meeting, take a few minutes on your own to process the information you learned. What are some specific steps that you can take to help your employee become more productive or effective at work?

PART III

ACCEPTANCE AND ACTION: FOCUSING ON OTHERS

*Treat people as if they were what they ought to be
and you help them become what they are capable of becoming.*

GOETHE

CHAPTER EIGHT

COACHING: A ONE-ON-ONE INTERACTION

In previous chapters, we identified the three essential qualities of grown-up leadership. Based on our experience, all great leaders work to improve their skills in each of these areas:

Maturity

Maturity requires the honesty, courage, and ability to examine and accept one's own fears and anxieties, then act with full consciousness of them. It is characterized by a centered, inner-directed (authentic), growth-motivated sense of security.

Versatility

Some leaders are naturally forceful, while others are more empowering. Exceptional leaders learn a variety of approaches and use those approaches to handle various situations. Moreover, they become able to use both styles seamlessly and authentically.

Relationship-Based Leadership

Beyond competency with tasks, leaders need to build strong relationships with those around them to achieve big picture objectives. This relational style, when balanced with strength, determination and openness, is encouraging and motivating to employees at all levels.

In our consulting practice, we observe that many who choose – or are chosen – to lead lack abilities in one, two, or all three areas. To truly grow up as a leader, you need to make considerable progress in each area. You must gain self-knowledge, become willing to try new behaviors, act to address weaknesses, and build on strengths. You will gain a lot by approaching learning as a vital process of your professional growth, welcoming input and taking risks along the way, and maintaining a positive outlook that keeps you focused on learning. By looking beyond your natural style and consciously adding new skills, you will take giant steps forward.

We said it earlier and will say it again: leadership is a technical specialty. Just as an engineer needs to master techniques to work with a wide range of materials, leaders need new sets of skills that will support both their forceful and empowering sides. Leaders must be able to develop and engage people, lead effective and results-oriented teams, and be lifelong learners.

GETTING THINGS DONE THROUGH OTHERS

As we've noted earlier, leaders accomplish results through other people.

Remember the football coach and the theater director, both of whom stand on the sidelines watching when the main events take place? They help us understand why effective leaders need maturity to develop the relational skills – and the versatility – to achieve success through others.

Beyond simply putting the right people on their teams, mature leaders need to get the most out of their employees, encouraging them to be as productive as possible. Enhancing productivity often means recognizing untapped potential. As a leader, your challenge is to share your experience and expertise with employees in ways that engage them and help them grow into the next generation of leaders.

ENGAGING THROUGH COACHING

By effective coaching, you can retain, engage, and grow your best employees. You can also deal with poor performance issues by identifying underlying causes of problems and devising effective solutions. Most important, you can help your team members prepare for the tasks that need to be accomplished when you are on the sidelines.

Many leaders fail to effectively engage their employees because they don't make coaching a high enough priority. We often see leaders in our coaching practice who get caught in activity traps, dealing with daily activities themselves, handling their own deadline-based work, or focusing on a stack of urgent projects that all demand immediate attention. They fall back on the same skill set they used in a previous position, and can't get beyond the piles on their desk. These individuals have hit a wall, and we hear them protest, "I'm busy all the time. When am I supposed to find the time to help other people grow?"

Let us remind you: There is no task more important to a leader than leading others. The best leaders among us are strategic thinkers, visionaries who think big and plan to achieve their vision. They know what the path ahead looks like and are able to convince others, saying, "Follow me, because I know where we are going." By communicating their vision over and over, both in small groups and in one-on-one interactions, leaders inspire team members to embrace the vision, which keeps all parts

---

WHEN LEADERS GET BUSY

HE SHE SAYS

Leigh Says

When Accommodators feel overwhelmed by the huge piles of work on their desks, they tend to disappear and avoid others. They may become inaccessible, stuck to their desks, or otherwise invisible or unreachable within the workplace. Busy Accommodators need to remind themselves to delegate tasks and reconnect with their co-workers. Share the load and come out of your cave!

Maureen Says

When Intimidators have too much on their plates, they sometimes forget about the relational side of leadership. They sometimes ignore the needs of their co-workers, drive people harder, and raise their expectations of others to unrealistic levels. Busy Intimidators need to listen to the messages they get from the people around them, and to keep in mind the human side of the workplace.

---

of the organization aligned.

Leaders whose daily work keeps them from executing through others are the ones who tend to remain stuck. They act as if they themselves will be playing the lead in the play on opening night, or like they will be starting at quarterback next Sunday. They haven't yet made the radical shift from a focus on tasks to a focus on relationships. They have yet to understand that they can accomplish their objectives better through other people.

So, are you stuck in a whirlwind of daily activities that keep you from successfully engaging your work team? Here are some questions to ask yourself if you need help in adjusting from an activity track to a leadership track:

- How can I make my people more knowledgeable and confident, and thus more productive?

- How can I provide my employees with opportunities to learn, grow, and feel more powerful in achieving our organization's success?
- How can I delegate work to free up my time for more important tasks?
- How can I shift my employees' expectations that I must always be involved when they could take responsibility and act on their own?

Coaching is one of the best investments leaders can make with their valuable time, because it focuses on helping their employees maximize professional performance. As a leader, you are responsible for developing the people that report to you, because ultimately your success will be judged by their abilities to perform. Coaching is the most important tool you can use to develop and drive employee performance and engagement. Simply put, leaders who cannot make time for coaching will not lead well.

The maturity, versatility, and interpersonal skills you've been developing as you've progressed through this book will now help you to:

- Drive and elicit excellence from employees.
- Create a motivating and engaging climate.
- Offer support and encouragement.
- Confront problems or deliver tough feedback when necessary.

So let's get started, coach!

CHALLENGES OF COACHING

Many leaders find coaching difficult. This reaction is understandable. Often, people earn promotions into leadership positions because they were excellent in executing tasks. They are not automatically prepared to sit down and talk to the people they lead. You've seen many examples of this – the star salesperson is a disaster as a vice president of sales, the brilliant accountant has half her staff leave in her first quarter as CFO.

COMMON CONCERNS ABOUT COACHING

This bears repeating: Every leader needs to set aside time for coaching. So when we hear some of these concerns, here's how we respond:

I don't have time for coaching.

Coaching is part of your job. If you can't make time for it, then you don't really want to be a leader, you want to be an individual contributor. All great leaders consider the development of people to be one of their top priorities because they recognize the role that those people play in realizing objectives.

I'm not qualified to coach my people.

For many, coaching is a learned skill. Perfection is not required before you start. As the Nike folks say, "Just Do It." You'll get better as you go. There are books, classes and seminars to help you learn, if you need to. We believe you'll improve dramatically simply by practicing the skills in this chapter.

I'm not a therapist. I don't do "touchy-feely."

We're not talking about therapy, but we *are* talking about connecting with your employees, which is an important part of your job as a leader. Discomfort is not an excuse to keep you from doing what you need to do: If you're uncomfortable with it, figure out why, and then take steps so you become more comfortable.

All the skills that you have learned and developed to this point, as well as all your leadership experience, will help you coach your people. Your newfound awareness and acceptance of your own tendencies and biases will help you understand and relate to those same tendencies and biases in your employees. The insight you've gained into your accommodating style, for example, will be a great tool when coaching an assistant manager who is also an Accommodator. Conversely, if the manager is an Intimidator, you can coach for versatility by citing contrasting examples from your own natural style.

Beyond time constraints, some leaders we work with simply avoid coaching because they feel quite uncomfortable in this setting.

Everyone can learn to become a better coach. In this chapter we will share examples, suggest guidelines, and help you develop a mindset for setting up engaging coaching sessions with your employees. We emphasize coaching approaches that encourage honesty, congruence, mutual respect, and understanding. Whether you are an Accommodator or Intimidator, whether your leadership style tends to be forceful or empowering, our suggestions will help you improve your coaching skills.

Practicing coaching

Are you ready to try coaching? Let's imagine that you will begin to coach two people on your team to help them become more effective as managers within your organization. Your job is to help, encourage, and motivate these two individuals – Allie the Accommodator and Ethan the Intimidator – to develop their own interpersonal skills in a way that will engage your workforce. Hopefully, these examples will apply to your real situation, and help you to consider ways to develop your skills, as well as the skills of people you lead.

Coaching Allie, the Accommodator

Allie brings many useful skills to her job, and has many effective qualities as a leader. Listening, supporting, and encouraging all come naturally to her. She is able to relate to the challenges others face because she is empathic – she connects well with others.

But leading is not only about being supportive. Leaders also need to motivate, a task that sometimes requires providing some forceful direction. And at times they need to confront problem behavior, which has been a real challenge for Allie. For her, growth means getting past her need to always be liked by her employees, and developing more self-confidence that others will respect. Beyond showing that she cares, there are times when Allie needs to be directive, and to take action if change isn't forthcoming.

Allie needs to outgrow her uncertainty and become more skillful at expressing her opinion *in the moment*. This means being more sponta- neous in conversations and in meetings rather than overanalyzing and editing her responses. Her current behavior confines her responses to those that she's absolutely certain are faultless and are politically cor- rect. The responses keep limiting her impact.

Speaking up: a development plan for Allie

As Allie's coach, you need to help her see how she can learn and prac- tice a new behavior. She needs help identifying practical steps that are part of a realistic development strategy. Suggest a personal development plan that she can use to learn the skills she needs. Through coaching sessions you can help her track her progress. Here are some recom- mendations you can make:

- Ask Allie to monitor her self-talk as a way to increase her awareness of her unedited, unexpressed thoughts and opinions.
- Encourage her to write down her ideas, to track and recognize them as they come up in meetings or conversations. Ask her to share these with you on a regular basis by e-mail, voicemail, or in person.
- Suggest that she set a goal of blurting out her ideas 25% more often in daily interactions with people.
- Work with her to create a means to follow up and track her progress on these activities.
- Recognize and encourage her as she progresses, but don't hesitate to point out flaws in what she thinks – in the way of honest feedback. False praise won't help.

Coaching Ethan, the Intimidator

We know that Intimidators are strong in addressing problems and pro- viding direction. In this case, Ethan's no-nonsense approach enables him to confront people, identify what needs to change, and clearly outline objectives.

Ethan's challenge is learning how to encourage his employees to succeed. To do this he will have to provide encouragement to employees, which requires more than being just a forceful task director. Ultimately, he needs to get better at connecting with them.

As Ethan's coach, you need to help him realize that simply telling people what he wants isn't enough in many instances. He also must outgrow his frustration, and develop patience to help some of his people get where they need to be. He needs to strengthen his listening, supporting and teaching skills.

Ethan also may feel frustrated at times and revert to thinking he needs new people who can accomplish tasks better. But that's not a logical process: first he must help his current team members see how they can each be more effective in their work.

Ethan must become more skillful at asking open-ended questions to better encourage his employees to share their perspectives on issues. He needs to learn to draw out their ideas and potential solutions so he can understand them better.

DRAWING OUT: A DEVELOPMENT PLAN FOR ETHAN

As Ethan's coach, you need to help him create a plan to facilitate his development. You might:

- Make sure Ethan knows what open-ended and closed questions are and how they *do* or *do not* draw people out (see pages 106–108).
- Ask Ethan to identify and write down three open-ended questions that he can use in meetings to draw out employee perspectives and ideas.
- Encourage Ethan to listen to employee thoughts without comment or criticism.
- Encourage Ethan to recognize and monitor his use of telling vs. asking; set a goal to increase asking by 25% and decrease telling by 25%.

Besides building development strategies for working with Allie and

Ethan, we recommend some additional action steps that will help them pursue their new objectives. Here are some practical ideas you might suggest to individuals that you coach:

- Observe two people who are already good at the behavior you are learning, to see what you can learn from them.
- Choose two or three colleagues to share your development plan with, and ask for their periodic feedback regarding your progress.
- Envision the improvement you are working towards by completing these thoughts:
  - I will know I have successfully learned this skill when...
  - When I have successfully learned this skill, others will observe ...

BECOMING A BETTER COACH

HE SHE SAYS

Leigh Says

As an Accommodator, I needed to learn to confront someone I'm coaching when they aren't following through with the tasks they have committed to. Accommodators can work so hard to be respectful that they don't hold people accountable when necessary. Stay focused on the objectives you have set, and let your people know when they aren't getting the job done.

Maureen Says

As an Intimidator, my instinct is to blurt out exactly what I see is wrong. I have learned to remind myself that it's best for my clients to come to conclusions themselves. We Intimidators are used to saying what we think, and often need to keep quiet in order to give people room to grow and expand in their own ways. Give them time and room, and you will get results.

THE LOGISTICS OF EFFECTIVE COACHING

By now, we hope we have convinced you about the need for you to coach effectively, as well as the benefits from making coaching a priority in your schedule. In addition, we hope our case studies of Allie and Ethan have helped you begin to understand what kinds of discussions you should have during your coaching meetings.

At this point, you may have more questions than answers about the kinds of conditions that can help make coaching work for you. We typically hear questions such as:

- What kinds of expectations should you set up prior to coaching an employee?
- How much should you take on with an employee?
- How often should you meet and for how long?

We recommend that you set up a specific coaching cycle with your key employees. This cycle clarifies expectations, gives structure to your sessions, helps you establish a flow of sharing and following up, and ensures that both you and your co-workers are committed to the process. Some coaching needs require frequent meetings, others may only need a quarterly check-up. Whatever you pick, make it realistic and keep committed to it. Here are some suggestions:

- Begin a coaching cycle with goal setting: Gather all members of your team together in order to review the company's goals and to agree on departmental goals.
- Then meet with employees individually to identify their own goals that will contribute to team goals. Make sure each goal is specific, measurable, achievable (yet suitably challenging), and relevant to their work. Set a time frame for each goal.
- Set up a regularly scheduled one-on-one meeting with each employee. (We suggest meeting at least once a month, more often if desired.)

- Use these coaching meetings to check on the status of projects, discuss concerns or issues that have arisen, and offer praise and/or constructive feedback as appropriate.
- At least once per quarter, use a regular coaching meeting to review progress on goals and to assess performance issues. Discuss project and development goals. Address questions such as:
  - What do you want to learn in the next three months?
  - What new relationships do you want to build in the next three months?
  - What talents would you like to use more?
  - What assignments or training will support your growth?

PRACTICALITIES OF COACHING

Nearly all our clients want to know the most practical information about coaching sessions. Here are our answers to the most frequently asked questions we hear, and specific coaching dos and don'ts:

- **How long should a coaching session last?** From 15 to 45 minutes, not longer.
- **What is the best location for coaching?** The best option is your office, but not seated behind your desk. You'll want to use the position power that comes from meeting in your office, but meet at a round table or at the edge of your desk to facilitate easy discussion. The second-best option is a neutral conference room, or any room with a door for privacy.
- **Do** consider coaching to be your highest priority work and treat it with as much respect as you would a key client contact. Start and end meetings on time. Create an agenda and expect both parties to come prepared. Schedule meetings on a regular day and time so you both get in the habit of keeping the time sacred.
- **Don't** answer your telephone during a meeting. And don't postpone or cancel a meeting with an employee unless it's an absolute emergency.

CREATING THE RIGHT MINDSET

Now that you've committed to setting up a coaching structure with your employees, it's time to focus on creating the conditions that will make your coaching sessions meaningful and worthwhile.

We work with our clients to develop a particular mindset concerning coaching. It's an approach that encourages employees to participate fully. We also teach specific learning and questioning skills that can be particularly valuable in coaching situations. The combination is extremely fruitful.

Becoming a better coach is a learning process. As we discussed, coaching is hard, and many of the skills required are not natural ones. As you read through the qualities we have outlined, consider ways in which you might practice new tactics in your one-on-one dialogues with employees.

You may find coaching to be a balancing act. You will need to learn how to select and use appropriate leadership styles that balance your twin objectives of developing and motivating people and achieving results. At the end of this chapter, our Personal Coaching Session exercise can help you do some pre-meeting planning and some post-meeting processing so that you can gain greater insight into your own skills and the areas in which you need to learn.

You will notice that the process creates trust and encompasses the presumption of good will. Effective engagement requires honest attempts at mutual understanding, which will remove concerns about office politics and encourage openness. The process encourages saying YES as much as possible.

As you meet with your employees, emphasize curiosity over judgment. This is a difficult area to work on, and you can expect to feel uncomfortable at first. Don't let that discomfort discourage you, because this is an important area, and one in which many leaders struggle. It will help you to remember that your goal is progress, not perfection. Your new capacities for accepting yourself will come in handy here, and feedback from employees should give you additional direction.

FOUR MINDSETS FOR POSITIVE COACHING ENVIRONMENTS

Mindset #1: Show Unconditional Respect and Positive Regard

- I start out with the assumption that I hold each employee in high esteem as a person.
- I may disagree with an employee's performance, opinions or values, yet respect him or her as a person.
- I start challenging comments with "With all due respect..."

Mindset #2: Listen with Empathy

- The employee talks.
- I listen.
- I ask open-ended questions. (See page 108.)
- I "step into" the employee's shoes.
- I am curious but not judgmental.
- I paraphrase the employee's statements, expressing both feeling and content.

Mindset #3: Act with Integrity

- I express my thoughts and feelings respectfully and directly.
- I walk the walk, not just talk the talk.
- I act true to my values.
- I speak about my values.

Mindset #4: Lead for Development

- I leverage the talents of each employee.
- I identify employee development desires and needs.
- I demonstrate versatile leadership (both forceful and empowering).

SKILLFUL LISTENING

Good listening skills are fundamental to leading and coaching. One reason listening is so difficult is that you can set the right conditions, use the right words and still have trouble communicating with your employees well, especially if you don't show you are listening. Body language plays a huge role, demonstrating that you are physically and emotionally present as a listener.

HOW TO SHOW YOU ARE ACTIVELY LISTENING

What you want to show		How show it?
Alertness	→	Make eye contact
Receptivity	→	Sit straight or lean forward
Interest	→	Nod
Concern	→	Use hand gestures
Involvement	→	Ask questions
Openness	→	Take notes

Use encouraging statements such as: "This is interesting." "Tell me more." "That's right."

You may pride yourself on your listening skills. To be sure you are in top form, check the "Don't" list on the next page and rank your performance. If you spot any shortcomings, try the remedies on the "Do" side.

SKILLFUL QUESTIONING

When you use questions to learn about the ideas and opinions of others, you encourage openness and engagement from your people. Questions have the ability to focus attention and increase our awareness. Use the power of asking instead of telling. You'll find a good question:

- Provides opportunity for learning both ways.
- Conveys respect and confidence in others.
- Creates openings for new ideas.
- Allows for exploration.

Open questions tend to give the other person room to roam. They require descriptive answers, promote awareness, and are much more effective in the coaching process for generating responsibility. Closed-ended or "yes/no" questions, while effective during cross-examinations,

DON'TS AND DO'S FOR LISTENING

Don't!

- Look bored, disinterested, or judgmental; avoid eye contact; turn your body away.
- Shift focus to yourself, talk about your own accomplishments.
- Fail to acknowledge the other person's ideas or feelings, make quick judgments, give unsolicited advice, lecture.
- Fail to see the other person's point of view or understand their feelings .
- Fail to ask follow-up questions to learn additional information, or ask only yes/no questions.
- Fail to check whether the message was received accurately.
- Narrow the choices by suggesting solutions too early in the discussion.
- Check your watch, answer your phone, scan emails while you are "listening."

Do!

- Make good eye contact, avoid distracting behavior, try to make your face expressive.
- Keep the focus of all comments on other person.
- Acknowledge and try to imagine the other person's ideas and feelings, probe for information before making recommendations.
- Ask open-ended questions to learn more and avoid jumping to conclusions.
- Restate what you think the other person said and keep broadening your understanding.
- Ask for ideas from the other person before providing alternatives.
- Allow the other person to pause, reflect, and formulate ideas before speaking.
- Clear you mind of your internal chatter and really focus on what the other person is saying.

are too absolute for accuracy, and they close the door on exploration of further dialogue. (In our list of examples, you'll also notice that we suggest avoiding questions that begin with the word "why," simply because they tend to encourage defensive reactions.)

OPEN AND CLOSED-ENDED QUESTIONS

Open-Ended Questions
(Encourage Elaboration)

- Can you tell me about what made that situation difficult?
- What were you thinking in that situation?
- What did you observe in the other person's response?
- How would you describe the encounter with your supervisor?

Closed-Ended Questions
(Discourage Elaboration)

- When did he say that?
- Were you frustrated when that happened?
- Who was at the meeting?
- Was your extra effort worthwhile?
- How many days will that take you to complete?

FINAL THOUGHTS

We began this chapter by recapping our three essential qualities of grown-up leaders. Now you may have noticed that all three qualities play key roles in effective coaching. They are intricately interconnected:

- To coach without judgment takes *maturity,*
- To successfully lead a variety of employees requires considerable *versatility,* and
- To effectively motivate others takes *relationship-building* skills.

All three require the ongoing commitment to learning and practicing that we have emphasized throughout this book.

In the next chapter, we will look at the task of leading teams, one of the most challenging roles that leaders play in organizations. The intricacies of group dynamics, individual motivations, and accomplishment of objectives make team leadership complex and fascinating. You can expect the task to require all of these essential qualities, as well as the coaching skills that you learned in this chapter.

DRIVING PRINCIPLES

- Coaching, a one-on-one process, plays a major role in engaging, motivating and directing employees. Successful leaders consider coaching one of their highest priorities.
- The ability to listen without judgment and ask insightful, open-ended questions that allow for learning and encourage forming of ideas is critically important for leaders.
- Effective leaders are able to create environments filled with conditions that encourage engaged employees.

Your Personal Coaching Session

Preparing for a Coaching Meeting

Holding regular coaching meetings will help you get better at coaching. The following exercise will help you by suggesting a process that you can use to prepare for and learn from these coaching meetings with your employees.

Before the meeting:

- Schedule an individual meeting with an employee.
- Set some goals for that meeting. How will you approach them? Make notes about questions that you want to ask. Pay attention to open-ended phrasing.
- Prepare for the meeting in advance, gathering any necessary data, such as feedback from other parties. You may ask your employee to prepare as well, such as by writing or thinking about answers to some questions that you pose.

During the meeting:

- Focus on the four mindsets of effective coaching (see page 105).
- Practice the listening and questioning skills in this chapter and stay focused on your employee.

Your Personal Coaching Session
(continued)

After the meeting:

- What did you notice about your behavior?
- How pleased were you with the process and outcomes?
- What did you think went well?
- What might you try to do differently in future meetings with that employee, or with other employees?
- What felt comfortable about this process?
- What felt uncomfortable about this process?
- How do you think the employee felt about the meeting? (Consider following up with them if you're not sure about the answer.)
- What next steps will you take to continue your coaching work with this person?

None of us
is as smart
as all of us.
KEN BLANCHARD

CHAPTER NINE

BUILDING AND LEADING
EFFECTIVE TEAMS

At the beginning of this book, we discussed the notion of being invited to sit at the grown-up table at family gatherings. After years spent with your siblings and cousins at the kid's table, your opportunity arrives and you get to eat with aunts and uncles, grandparents and adult friends. But the question is, now that you have arrived at the grown-up table, how do you need to behave?

As viewed from the kids' table, the grown-up table can seem pretty functional – adults can talk with each other, laugh, share ideas, and tell stories. But some grown-up tables are actually pretty dysfunctional places, complete with Intimidators who bully and disparage others, Accommodators who harbor silent resentments, and loads of people fighting for attention. You sense unspoken expectations, see unhealthy habits, and generally feel the strain of immaturity. When you end up at a table like that, you might yearn for the fun of the kids' table.

Since this is a book about leadership, let's take this analogy one step farther. Let's suppose that you have been appointed as the leader of the group seated at the grown-up table. In our practice, we think of teams within an organization as groups of adults sitting around grown-up tables. Some teams are highly functional, vibrant, exciting, and capable; others are childish, petty, and downright frustrating, not to mention ineffective. Leading these teams calls on all of the abilities, skills, and knowledge that we've discussed in this book thus far.

Team leadership can be difficult, as you may have experienced. An autocratic or forceful style can help a team get launched, but may inhibit its evolution into a productive group. An empowering style may leave it without the rudder that is needed to get it moving in the right direction in early team meetings. Leaders need to have some of the answers to team issues, but leaders who believe they have all of the answers can foster apathy and resentment among team members.

The purpose of this chapter is to help you understand the dynamics of team leadership. In it we will offer you core knowledge, wisdom, experience, and expertise regarding how you can build and lead functional and productive teams in your organization. Almost every topic we've previously discussed in this book will contribute to your ability to successfully lead a team. Leading a group requires a synthesis of all the skills you have learned to date:

- The self-awareness and confidence that comes from maturity. It will help you overcome the difficulties of forming a group.
- Your understanding of Ellis' structure of interpretation (see Chapter 2). It will help you to recognize prisms and motivations of individual team members (including your own) and address issues appropriately.
- Your versatility. It will be more important than ever, because the natural stages of a team's evolution will require you to use both forceful and empowering styles as the situation demands.
- Your relationship-based leadership skills. They will be vital to understanding and handling group dynamics, dealing with conflict, and

keeping your team engaged, motivated, and on course.

- Your coaching skills. They will help you to stay connected with your team, encourage communication, and remain a motivating and engaging presence.

WHAT IS A TEAM?

Think once again about the football coach and the theater director. As leaders, they clearly need to accomplish things through the people that they lead. Ultimately, as a team leader, you – like them – are responsible for your team's performance. You hold a high stake in the team's success. It's critically important for you to have a vision of how your team will accomplish its ultimate objectives. But you must achieve this vision through motivating and encouraging others. This, frankly, is quite a challenge for even the best leaders among us.

Before we proceed, let's clarify what we mean by a "team." In most organizational settings, a team is a group of people who must work together in order to accomplish a specific purpose, one which they all presumably care about and agree upon.

Some groups or teams exist mostly because everyone reports to the same manager. The team members' roles do not overlap much, and team meetings are mostly opportunities for information sharing and looking for opportunities to share resources. If you are leading this type of team, your job is easier – your primary job is to make certain that you run good meetings, facilitate sharing of data and ideas, and seize opportunities to manage the group efficiently.

Organizations and leaders also form teams to accomplish objectives that none of the members could accomplish on their own. An example might be a team formed to create a new manufacturing process. As the team leader, your objective won't be realized unless you can build a productive group. So your job goes well beyond thinking about manufacturing – you are challenged to:

- Help team members build productive relationships with each other.

- Draw out and resolve differences about how to accomplish the task.
- Create an environment where team members are motivated and excited about their work and take responsibility for contributing their best efforts.
- Encourage innovation.
- Guide the team through the larger organization that you serve.

ENVIRONMENTAL INFLUENCES THAT AFFECT TEAMS

No team operates in a vacuum. We recognize that there are many outside influences that can affect how a team carries out its work. In a perfect world, we should empower teams to operate as their own indepen-

---

ROADBLOCKS TO TEAM EFFECTIVENESS

Most teams typically encounter one or more potential barriers to operating effectively. Good leaders can help their teams navigate around barriers such as:

Being too big: Teams that have more than eight members almost always have problems making decisions. This is because effective teams make most (not all) decisions by consensus. Trying to get more than eight people to agree on one best decision is extraordinarily difficult.

Limited commitment: It is not enough to want to work together. The effort and personal risk involved in building an effective team will only be undertaken by team members who realize that the purpose and goals they care about can best be accomplished by working together.

Unclear purpose: This is a recipe for frustration and low team effectiveness. Try an experiment. Ask each member of your team to independently jot down your team's purpose in one or two sentences. If their answers are not the same, each team member is trying to accomplish a different purpose.

---

dent entities as much as possible. But this is not the typical situation. External influences often become barriers to a team's success.

Team leaders need to assume the task of examining systems outside of the team that may impact their work. Failure to do so can substantially limit your effectiveness. Consider these examples of how outside influences affect teams:

- **Too much attention.** A product development team in the medical devices industry has been working on an important and innovative product to bring to market. The initial results have become so impressive that the CEO has taken an even greater interest in the team's work, and now considers the device his "pet project." Both leader and members are feeling a greater amount of pressure, and are concerned that the CEO will become the real decision-maker in their group.
- **Too little attention.** Team A shares key members with Team B, which is led by a more senior company leader. The shared members are clearly investing more time and energy in their work with Team B. As a result, Team A's meetings are poorly attended, resulting in poor progress towards its goals.
- **Unhealthy competition.** A sales team at a printing company has become so successful that some of its members have begun to look down on their colleagues on other sales teams. This elitism has become a problem within the company, fueling resentments and potentially affecting the quality of the company's work. Yet the owner needs the "numbers" that this team has been able to generate, and is hesitant to take any action that would affect their productivity.
- **Inadequate resources.** A team really needs an engineer who can fill a key role, but the engineering department is running lean, and the individual assigned isn't able to fully participate in the team's work.

Team leaders need to recognize and address outside factors that will impact their ability to function. This means ensuring that team members

---

BUILDING TEAM COMMITMENT

One way to build commitment among your team members is to work at team build-ing. Try inviting team members to privately answer two questions:

1. On a scale of one (low) to seven (high), how much coordination and collabo-ration is required in order to achieve our purpose?
2. On the same scale of one (low) to seven (high), how effective is our team work today?

Then, ask each team member to explain their answer to each question and the rea-son for their answers. If team members feel a need to work on team building, most will agree that improving their teamwork will raise the quality of work currently being done by the team.

---

are able to commit to the team, that the appropriate skills are repre-sented, that adequate resources are available to accomplish its goal, and that the appropriate levels of organizational authority are present within the team.

A MODEL FOR TEAM EFFECTIVENESS

To build an effective team, you need to address three primary objectives:

- Structuring your team for success
- Building commitment for team building among the members
- Discussing and agreeing on the elements of your team's effective-ness model

As a team leader, you play a key role in achieving these objectives. Be-yond that, you need to understand qualities of group dynamics in order to effectively guide teams. This understanding will help you recognize what types of leadership skills will be most useful to the team in different situations. Groups, like people, evolve over time, with different leadership tactics and styles effective at different points in their life cycles.

Some focused "pre-work" will help you to avoid the barriers to success that we discussed. First, you must reorganize as required so that your team is appropriately sized. Second, you must consider the team's role within a larger context and make any adjustments in that external context that can limit your group's effectiveness. We also suggest drafting an initial statement of your team's purpose, which the team should examine at one of your first meetings. This purpose statement will be discussed and modified by the whole team, but it is your job to provide a starting point for discussion.

To help you better understand dynamics of team building, let us examine some of the factors that combine to create engaged and productive teams. Richard Beckhard, and later James Shonk, described a "Team Effectiveness Model" that we find helpful in understanding these dynamics. At its core, team effectiveness involves a process of creating, and then continually refining, the following team success factors: *vision, mission, goals, roles, processes,* and *relationships*. In this section we will explain these factors, and suggest ways that as a grown-up leader, you can help your team excel in these six critical areas.

1. VISION: DEFINING SUCCESS

Vision articulates success. A team's vision should describe, as specifically as possible, what team success looks like. The purpose of vision is to motivate team members towards greater effort and achievement, and to align team members towards a common definition of success. Vision is like the North Star, offering both direction and inspiration.

A team actually needs two visions for success. The first describes successful results. For example, a team creating a new brand identity might define a successful result as gaining a clear understanding of how the company is perceived by its key stakeholders and developing a focused plan for reaching high potential prospects.

The second vision describes how the team wants to work together. Each team member will bring to the team his or her previous experiences with working on teams.

In an effective team,

- Team members share a vision of how they will work together.
- Team members agree what success looks like.

What grown-up leaders do to support a team's vision

Early in the team's life, spend time asking each team member to describe his or her best team experience. As each team member describes his or her "personal best," listen for similar themes that all can agree on for how the team you are creating should work together. That way, you can be certain that all team members are committed to creating a shared team experience, rather than having each team member trying to re-create his or her own personal definition of effective team work.

2. Mission: team purpose

Mission describes specifically the reason for the team's existence. In order to define its mission, or purpose, you need to help the team answer the following questions:

- **What?** What specifically does the team produce? Some teams produce tangible products (such as medical devices), services (such as accounting or consulting services), or functions, like sales teams do. Others might have short-term lives, as for example a cross-functional task force that could be charged with creating a position paper, outlining a new process or operating principles, developing budgets or strategies, or planning a company picnic. Teams also deliver less tangible "products" such as enhanced understanding between employees from different parts of a company. This can be especially challenging if great distances, different time zones, and multiple cultures come into play.

- **Who?** For whom does the team produce its products, services or outcomes? Who are your team's key customers and stakeholders?

- **How?** What unique production methods or processes are employed in creating the team's output?

- **Why?** What personal reasons do team members have for feeling passionate about producing the team's output?

In an effective team,

- The mission is understood by all members.
- It is aligned with the mission of the larger organization.

What grown-up leaders do to clarify a team's mission

It's vital to facilitate group dialogue that will help team members shape and understand the team's mission. Be sure to get everyone involved in the discussion, because incomplete or poor understanding of the mission, or disagreements about the scope of the team's work, can inhibit its progress.

3. Goals: what progress looks like

Vision and mission are important for pointing a group in a single, agreed direction. Goals provide a mechanism for measuring whether the group is making progress in that direction. Think about taking a road trip with your friends or family. Assume your destination (or vision) is San Francisco, California. If you start out from New York City, you might set a goal of reaching Indianapolis for your first night. Now, imagine if this first night's goal had not been discussed in advance, and the driver instead takes the road to Nashville. Group frustration often results from a lack of team unity regarding the road map. The ability of a group to formulate goals and agree on means and measures of progress toward them is critical for a team's success.

In an effective team,

- Members are involved in setting goals.
- Goals are understood and agreed with by all members.
- Goals are set and met within realistic time frames.

What grown-up leaders do to clarify a team's goals

> A person is not given integrity. It results from the reluntless pursuit of honesty at all times.
>
> Unknown

Encourage lively discussions and even debates to reach agreements about team goals. Work to ensure that goals are realistic, and encourage members to fully commit to understanding and achieving those goals. Build and maintain team morale by measuring progress towards team goals, and plan for celebrations when you achieve certain landmarks.

4. Roles: who does what

Once team goals are established, each member needs to know his or her role within the team, and specifically what he or she can do to contribute to achieving the goals. Different from job descriptions, roles are the result of a negotiation between each team member and the rest of the team.

Team members often have unexpressed expectations for each other, which need to be aired, discussed, and clarified. Failing to clarify expectations can lead to frustration, mistrust, and the failure to accomplish important tasks.

In an effective team,

- Roles are well defined and don't overlap.
- Team members and leaders clearly understand and accept them.
- Team members and leaders accept the tasks and assignments that fit their roles.
- Members and leaders are accessible and help each other.

WHAT GROWN-UP LEADERS DO TO CLARIFY TEAM MEMBERS' ROLES

It's very important for you to clarify your own role as leader of the team, regarding such things as your role in team meetings, resolving disagreements, and making decisions. Failure to define your role can affect team development and even lead to power plays for authority. As leader, you must have clearly defined responsibilities, especially in the early stages (more on this later), and you must also help team members understand their own roles as the team evolves.

5. PROCESSES: ACCOMPLISHING THE TEAM'S WORK

Whether they are discussed and agreed to or just happen, processes develop as teams work together. Processes are the rules a team uses for meetings and individual member interactions. Explicitly discussing and agreeing on your team's processes, rather than simply letting them evolve into less-than-constructive behaviors, will increase the likelihood that your team will effectively accomplish its mission.

In an effective team,

- Decision-making is timely, involving the appropriate team members.
- Meetings are efficient, with an emphasis on solving problems.
- Discussions proceed with all members listening and participating.
- Members stay informed via minutes and other communications.
- All members establish and keep deadlines and milestones.

WHAT GROWN-UP LEADERS DO TO SUPPORT A TEAM'S PROCESSES

You will need to help your team set up ground rules, and gain group agreement on those rules, in order to keep meetings effective and support productivity. Be clear about expectations about attendance, timeliness, and enforcement of ground rules. You'll also need to lead the group in deciding how decisions will be made. Make sure you abide by the rules: some team leaders are the busiest members, and are the ones most likely to show up late or miss a deadline.

6. RELATIONSHIPS: THE QUALITY OF TEAM MEMBER INTERACTIONS

In order to function effectively, team members must respect each other and be able to speak openly and honestly with each other. This does not mean that team members must be best friends.

Most often, when team member relationships are strained, the reason has less to do with personality conflicts than with disagreements or lack of clarity about team vision, purpose, goals, roles, and processes. The lack of clarity results in frustration, and relationships can deteriorate quickly.

Paradoxically, the solution to strained relationships and low trust is not to go bowling or have a pizza party (not that these can't be fun). When relationships are strained, a more successful approach generally involves reviewing the team's vision, purpose, and goals and looking for misunderstandings, disagreements, or lack of clarity.

In an effective team,

- Relationships flourish: team identity and pride are evident.
- Members show tolerance for conflict, with emphasis on resolution.
- Members enjoy (or appreciate) and support each other.
- Conflict leads to growth or learning.

WHAT GROWN-UP LEADERS DO TO SUPPORT TEAM RELATIONSHIPS

By being a leader who works to ensure a group focus on mission and vision and by clarifying goals, process and roles, you will help your team members build good relationships. Competition and personality conflicts can get in the way of achieving team goals. You can take specific steps to keep everyone on task, such as modeling mature leadership styles and coaching individual team members to both participate and perform.

If you follow the discipline of working through these steps, we guarantee you that you'll see improved teamwork.

DRIVING PRINCIPLES

- Different personalities bring unique sets of skills to their roles as team leaders.
- Leaders hold a high stake in their team's success, but must achieve success through motivating and encouraging others.
- As a grown-up leader, you need vision of how your team will succeed.
- Effective teams are characterized by vision, important and meaningful missions, accepted leadership, clarity of goals, clarity of roles, and solid relationships.

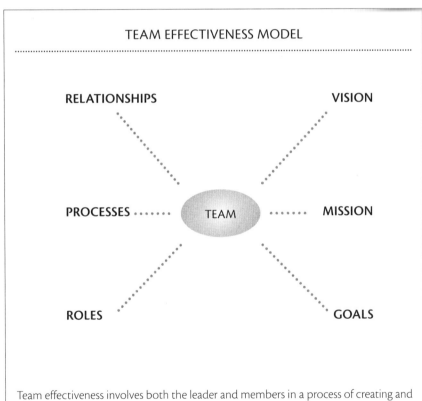

TEAM EFFECTIVENESS MODEL

RELATIONSHIPS   VISION

PROCESSES .... TEAM .... MISSION

ROLES   GOALS

Team effectiveness involves both the leader and members in a process of creating and then continually refining these six critical success factors.

Your Personal Coaching Session

Defining Team Processes

All teams have group processes. Some of those processes simply evolve after a few meetings, and aren't always helpful to the team's work. If people don't arrive on time, for example, then an expectation builds that members can show up late. Similarly, if certain members don't attend, and that issue isn't dealt with, then other members may begin to consider the meetings optional.

Effective leaders will help their teams consciously examine processes instead of letting processes evolve unchecked. Team processes include norms (or ground rules), decision-making expectations, and meeting protocols. Take some time with your team to define these processes as a group, making adjustments as necessary. Encourage your members to commit to them through future team meetings and activities.

Team norms: Team norms are basic ground rules to be followed when the team meets. Once the norms are agreed to, the team should review them at the beginning of each of its meetings, and also use them for periodic evaluation of how well the team is doing in following the norms. Your norms should number between six and eight, and might include statements such as:

- Show up to meetings or send a "proxy" in your place (assuming the team has decided about the acceptability of proxies).
- Be on time.
- Listen for understanding.
- Resolve conflicts.
- Before making decisions, discuss how the decision will be made (see below).

Your Personal Coaching Session
(continued)

Decision making: Team members often make the error of believing that all team decisions must be made by consensus. Reaching consensus requires that every team member has his or her say and feels heard, and that a decision has been reached that all can agree and commit to. It is time consuming, sometimes impossible, and not always the best strategy. Effective teams make most decisions through discussion, negotiation and agreement, but also recognize that there are times when a decision needs to be made by the team leader or delegated to a subset of the entire team. What is most important is that teams talk about how to make important decisions before actually deciding.

Team meetings: At the beginning of their team's life, and periodically thereafter, team members should discuss how meetings will be run. Important considerations include:

- How often will the team meet?
- What days and times will meetings be held?
- Who will set the agenda for meetings?
- How much time in meetings will be reserved for team problem solving and how much for status updates?
- What does the team expect of members in terms of their preparation before a meeting?
- Who will facilitate the meetings?
- What happens if the agenda is not completed by the end of the time scheduled for the meeting?
- How will notes of the meeting be kept?

Teamwork is the quintessential contradiction
of a society grounded
in individual achievement.

MARVIN R. WEISBORD

CHAPTER TEN

GROWN-UP LEADERSHIP: MANAGING GROUP DYNAMICS

Most seasoned leaders find that learning about group dynamics enhances their leadership skills. Leaders who understand how teams develop over time, and what teams need from their leaders during different stages of development, are better prepared to help them succeed.

STAGES OF TEAM DEVELOPMENT

Here's a dynamic that we find most helpful, which has been supported by numerous studies. Teams typically evolve through four stages: they form, storm, norm, and perform. We should note that teams that get stuck in one stage too long will have trouble achieving any of their goals. Each stage is accompanied by an increase in team productivity.

As we define each stage of team development, we'll share some characteristics of that stage, and also show how your maturity, versatility, and relational skills can help you navigate these stages and help your team gain confidence, effectiveness, and productivity.

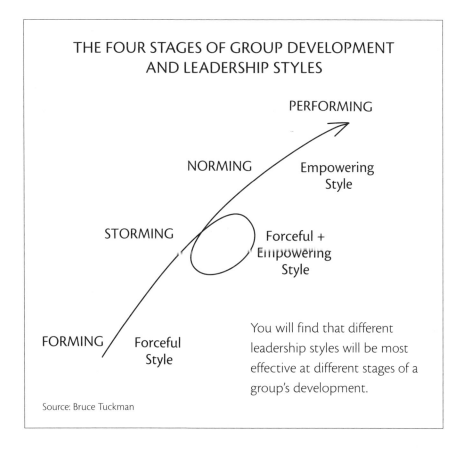

THE FOUR STAGES OF GROUP DEVELOPMENT
AND LEADERSHIP STYLES

PERFORMING

NORMING   Empowering
                   Style

STORMING   Forceful +
                   Empowering
                   Style

FORMING   Forceful   You will find that different
           Style   leadership styles will be most
                          effective at different stages of a
                          group's development.

Source: Bruce Tuckman

STAGE 1: FORMING – ORIENTATION TO GROUP AND TASK

This first stage of a group's development often feels somewhat uncomfortable and leader-dominated. Members can be reluctant to contribute during Forming, causing quiet meetings that feel inefficient. Your role as a leader is to facilitate participation from all members, assign roles and tasks as needed, and persevere in communicating the team's role and value. By the end of the Forming stage, members have to agree on the team's vision, mission, goals, and members' roles, and share an understanding of how the team will proceed.

During Forming, you will find that our qualities of grown-up leadership apply in these ways:

MATURITY: The Forming stage requires a great deal of patience and understanding from you. All eyes are on you as a leader. Team members are looking to you for guidance and direction. Thus, meetings may seem leader-dominated. Your self-confidence is also important at this stage, because members offer you very little feedback, and it can be a lonely time to lead.

VERSATILITY: A forceful leadership style is most effective during group formation. The reason is that team members are not yet ready to contribute fully – they are concerned about being judged or rejected by others, and feel unsure of their roles. During Forming, an empowering style is inappropriate because the team is not yet ready to assume any decision-making responsibilities. As a leader, you must provide structure by preparing agendas in advance and articulating the group's purpose.

RELATIONSHIP-BASED LEADERSHIP: Relational skills are vital at this stage. They encourage participation among all group members. Your challenge will be to draw out the Accommodators while moderating the dominance of the Intimidators.

STAGE 2: STORMING – CONFLICT OVER CONTROL AMONG MEMBERS AND LEADER

During Storming, team members start to become more visible, testing your authority as a leader, challenging ideas, and trying to make their own impacts on the team. If you are a leader who is uncomfortable with conflict, this can be a difficult stage. But healthy disagreement is very helpful during Storming, and your role in working through the conflict is pivotal.

During Storming, you will find that our qualities of grown-up leadership apply in these ways:

MATURITY: You will need to resist the temptation to shut down conflict. Rather, recognize it as an important part of the group's evolution. Relationships will evolve, competition will develop, and tension will rise. Your role is to help bring unspoken conflict to the surface, and to help facilitate discussions around them. That process is critical in helping your team move through this stage and gradually shift interpersonal tensions toward a desire to get tasks done.

VERSATILITY: The forceful leadership style that existed during Forming should be tempered a bit during Storming. You need to remain forceful, but begin to recognize and seize opportunities to empower others within the group. You will be watched closely as you do this. Be aware that concerns about workload and size of tasks are likely to arise as team members struggle to organize themselves.

CHALLENGING THE WILL OF THE GROUP

Sometimes a group member – or even a group leader – believes that their own idea or strategy will be a better solution than the one the group has reached together. This presents a challenge: if you are the one who disagrees, should you go along with what you believe to be an inferior solution, for the good of the group?

Disagreement does not have to alienate group members from each other. The way you present your ideas may be as important as the ideas themselves. We've seen people offer their input with a condescending, "I know better" attitude that is certainly harmful to the group. But if ideas are suggested (or challenged) in a more open manner, the team process can tolerate disagreement more effectively.

It is important to show that you respect the team's common welfare. For example, if you think they are missing an obvious solution to a problem, you might ask open-ended questions that logically reflect on the group's assumptions behind the decision. If you have additional information that should be considered, take the opportunity to share what you know and encourage members to reconsider. If you really disagree, state your case as best you can and then trust the group's process. Strong teams can handle that kind of input.

RELATIONSHIP-BASED LEADERSHIP: Relationships can fluctuate during Storming, with the potential for team members to become polarized. You should facilitate open discussions, ask questions, and encourage listening among members. This is a good time to share your knowledge on open-ended questions and listening skills, perhaps tying them to your team's process agreements. You may need to do some coaching with individual members outside of the group to encourage participation or resolve issues.

STAGE 3: NORMING – TEAM FORMATION AND SOLIDARITY

As teams gel during Norming, they begin to feel pleased with their accomplishments and enjoy the company of their colleagues. Members typically begin to recognize the greater good of the team is more important than their own individual agendas. In some cases, members may believe that they have reached their peak. At this point, you need to keep your team focused and on task, encouraging members to continue to challenge each other, using tools to further motivate the team, and keeping the team development moving into the fourth stage, Performing, where teams achieve real excellence.

During Norming, you will find that our qualities of grown-up leadership apply in these ways:

MATURITY: Since processes are generally well established by Norming, and group cohesiveness is more evident, it's time for you now to let go of control, and let the team members start to shine. You should openly share issues or concerns, delegate management tasks, and work behind the scenes to keep people focused.

VERSATILITY: A forceful leader may have difficulty during Norming. You will do more good for your team by sitting back and reflecting about the group's direction. But you may still need to use a forceful style to keep the team focused, because newly-developed cohesiveness can lead to conflict avoidance and reduced innovation.

RELATIONSHIP-BASED LEADERSHIP: Now is the time to challenge the group to be more open about issues and concerns, offer and request constructive feedback about the team, and encourage others to take on leadership roles. As Norming continues, successful team leaders find they lead mainly through empowering other team members.

STAGE 4: PERFORMING –
GROUP DIFFERENTIATION AND PRODUCTIVITY

Stage four, Performing, is the ultimate goal for your team. Teams that reach this stage are highly productive and effective: members thrive within their roles, encourage each other to excel, commit high levels of energy to their tasks and accomplish challenging goals. In short, they perform outstanding work, both in quality and quantity. At this point, your role as leader is to consistently challenge your team; examine and assess their mission, goals and processes; engage the individual members; share credit; and keep the team focused on team objectives. If you do this, you will successfully lead a high performance team.

During Performing, you will find that our qualities of grown-up leadership apply in these ways:

MATURITY: A selfless, encouraging leadership style will serve the team best at the Performing stage. You have accomplished a great deal by leading your team this far, and you now need to fully let go of the reigns and trust the group, recognize the contributions of team members, and encourage members to continue to grow and develop. As the team becomes its own functional entity, it can be more productive than ever.

VERSATILITY: By the time a team reaches Performing, you can safely assume a fully empowering style. Take the opportunity to empower your team members in new ways. Look for opportunities to increase the team's scope, choose a role that is interesting to you, and build links to the outside organization. You can also start to turn your own attention to new priorities.

Relationship-based leadership: Nevertheless, you should continue to coach and develop team members for future roles, inside and outside the team. It may also be necessary to plan how to manage the team's disbanding if its objectives have been achieved, or help it prepare for any future adjustment to its tasks.

> A leader is best when people barely know he exists. When his work is done, his aim is fulfilled, they will say: We did it ourselves.
>
> Lao Tzu

As you can see, guiding your team will take all of your leadership skills – both those that feel natural and those that you are learning. As your team evolves, you will need to be able to be both forceful and empowering at times. Through maturity, versatility and personal connections, you will have the flexibility you need to respond as situations warrant. You'll use your ability to both connect and detach as necessary. You'll recognize when to challenge or encourage, and use your capacity to motivate and influence team members.

DRIVING PRINCIPLES

- Team leaders can be more effective when they understand group dynamics and the stages of a team's life: Forming, Storming, Norming and Performing.
- While grown-up leadership skills are important at each stage of a team's development, different stages call for different skills.
- Forceful leadership is often needed in the early stages; encouraging leadership comes more into play during the later stages.

Your Personal Coaching Session

Enhancing Team Effectiveness

Scheduling periodic team effectiveness meetings can help many teams to establish direction or renew energy. Plan a meeting with a team that you currently work with to help set, review or refocus your efforts. Follow our suggested agenda, inviting team members to answer the questions in any format that is comfortable (e.g., bullet points, statements, paragraphs, or individual words).

As the team leader, part of your job is to keep members focused on this agenda. Ensure that everyone gets a chance to participate, and that there is consensus at the end of this process.

Team-effectiveness meeting agenda

As a group, answer the following questions:

- What makes our team's mission exciting, meaningful, and important?
- How does our team contribute to the overall success of our company?
- What are our top five goals to measure success this year? (Make sure your goals are SMART: Specific, Measurable, Achievable, Relevant, and Time-bound)
- At what stage of development (Forming, Storming, Norming, Performing) is our team operating? How do we know?
- What action(s) must we take to move to the next stage?

Never doubt that a small group of thoughtful,
committed citizens can change the world; indeed,
it's the only thing that ever has.

MARGARET MEAD

CHAPTER ELEVEN

THE RIPPLE EFFECT

Recently, one of our clients, having successfully navigated through many of the ideas and exercises we've presented in this book, asked us if we believe that leaders recognize and understand the need for maturity and versatility in their jobs. Do most leaders see that a lack of self-awareness is a major barrier to their success?

Our honest response: No, there are not enough grown-up leaders out there in the world today. As long as any given roomful of people can easily come up with a long laundry list of immature leadership characteristics drawn from their personal experiences, we know that more leaders need to learn these principles. And, as we've said before, the people working for them deserve mature leaders.

Our client replied, "I'd like to go out and teach my colleagues and employees about your principles of grown-up leadership." Needless to say, that struck us as a noble and attractive idea.

But remember, while we all have big aspirations, we must remember that mastery begins at home. We certainly encourage you to share your learning experiences with others, or perhaps to discuss this book with them. But even if you don't do that, you'll find that your own grown-up leadership has a ripple effect. People notice it, respond well to it, and make changes for the better, thanks to your own growth.

DOING VS. TEACHING

In other words, you don't need to teach grown-up leadership – you need to *do* it. Because when you practice grown-up leadership, you are being authentic, and you invite authentic responses in return. When you demonstrate an ability to support, motivate, *and* direct, for example, your co-workers will recognize your inner confidence, capability, and skill. When a team you lead accomplishes a major objective or performs at a superior level for an extended period of time, those around you will notice your accomplishment. In this way your growth inspires the growth of others.

You'll see it. People will respond to your grown-up approach. They will reward you with loyalty, trust, and welcome your continued leadership. And, following their own timetables, many of them will take some of the same steps that you are taking to grow up, personally and professionally. As you lead and coach others, you will find appropriate times to encourage your employees to begin their own process of becoming grown-up leaders.

Here's another way to describe this ripple effect: Your awareness and acceptance of your own strengths and weaknesses will help you take actions that will make you a more mature and versatile leader. This focus on your *self* will positively impact your individual work relationships with the people around you as you become a more effective coach. These new relational skills, in turn, will improve your ability to lead teams around you to achieve at the highest levels possible.

CONTINUING THE PROCESS

As you certainly have seen by now, grown-up leadership is a process, not an event. Even after you become aware of your own prisms and beliefs, for example, you will find that they continue to affect your actions,

THE RIPPLE EFFECT OF GROWN-UP LEADERSHIP

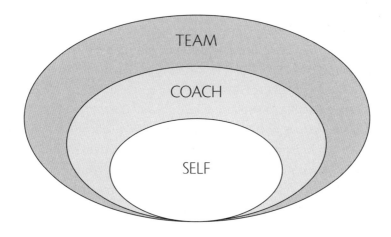

TEAM

COACH

SELF

You don't need to call attention to your self-development. Others will notice its effects and probably will comment on the changes you have made. Your increasing maturity, versatility, and ability to build relationships will make you a more successful coach and team leader, and people you work with will see the improved results you deliver.

despite the fact that you are aware of them. After all, you've been (un)consciously maintaining them for years. Through practice, you will learn to disregard them more often when they present barriers, but they won't go away for some time, if ever.

You can expect your accommodating or intimidating tendencies to continue to pop up from time to time, too. Please don't be discouraged – this process is a normal part of growing up. Remaining grown up as a leader requires an ongoing willingness to stay connected to yourself and the people around you. As you continue down this path, challenging your beliefs and actively practicing new behaviors, you – and those around you – will encounter the Accommodator or Intimidator in their extreme forms of behavior less frequently.

We encourage grown-up leaders to continually look for ways to grow as adults. The Personal Coaching Sessions in this book give you exercises that you can return to regularly to reassess your situation, or to confront a particular issue you face. Keep setting personal and professional objectives, and make plans to revisit them regularly.

THE FUTURE OF LEADERSHIP

What's the ultimate benefit of grown-up leadership? By learning to be mature, versatile, and relational, you bring qualities to your workplace that are desperately needed both today and in the future. Many of today's largest and most successful companies are allocating significant time and money trying to solve their leadership challenges. We believe that if you adopt and practice the ideas this book offers, your leadership will help your organization excel.

Here's why. As organizations increasingly value innovation, creativity, *and* bottom-line accountability, they count on grown-up leaders to help them balance motivation, encouragement, and expectations. They need team players who can be both forceful and empowering, who can overcome personal demons to deal with people in mature ways, and who can effectively motivate people and groups to perform at the peak of their abilities.

Grown-up leaders will be the people best equipped to meet such complex demands. We congratulate you on starting this journey!

DRIVING PRINCIPLES
- By "doing" or modeling grown-up leadership, you have a positive impact on those around you.
- Grown-up leaders continually set personal and professional goals, and revisit them regularly.
- As the business climate becomes increasingly complex, organizations need grown-up leaders more and more in order to succeed.

Making an Appointment with Yourself

At least once a week, make some time to stop at a coffee shop, café, bakery or other relaxing spot on your way to work. Block out about 45 minutes and use that time to plan your day or week, write in a journal, read something uplifting or inspirational (not a newspaper or work memo), or just sit quietly while enjoying your private time.

We suggest doing this weekly for at least six weeks. The repetition will help you develop the discipline of protecting this quality time, a small personal retreat where you won't be harassed by phone calls, e-mails or office clutter.

Here's how our clients have benefited from this exercise:

- They become more purposeful.
- Their priorities get clearer.
- They use personal time more efficiently.
- Their perspectives on challenges seem more positive.
- They find more creative solutions, more easily.

Both introverts and extroverts appreciate this down time, and report feeling happier and better about themselves as a result. This is a perfect example of how spending time with yourself leads to personal growth and greater effectiveness as a leader. So enjoy the experience, and continue the process of becoming a grown-up leader.

BIBLIOGRAPHY

GENERAL LEADERSHIP

Collins, Jim. *Good to Great.* Harper Business, 2001.

Gardner, Howard. *Leading Minds: An Anatomy of Leadership.* Basic-Books, 1996.

McGregor, Douglas. *The Human Side of Enterprise.* McGraw Hill, 1960.

Rucci, Anthony J., Steven P. Kirn and Richard T. Quinn. "The Employee-Customer-Profit Chain." *Harvard Business Review* (January-February, 1998, pp. 82-98).

PSYCHOLOGICAL TYPES

Briggs Myers, Isabel and Peter B. Myers. *Gifts Differing.* Consulting Psychologists Press, Inc., 1980.

Campbell, Joseph. *The Portable Jung.* Penguin Books, 1971.

Dunne, Claire. *Carl Jung: Wounded Healer of the Soul.* Continuum Books, 2000.

Hirsh, Sandra and Jean Kummerow. *LIFETypes.* Warner Books, Inc., 1989.

MATURITY

Beattie, Melody. *Codependent No More.* Harper and Row Publishers, Inc., 1987.

Chödrön, Pema. *The Wisdom of No Escape.* Shambala Publications, Inc., 1991.

Chödrön, Pema. *When Things Fall Apart.* Shambala Publications, Inc., 1997.

Ellis, Albert. *How to Make Yourself Happy and Remarkably Less Disturbable.* Impact Publishers, Inc., 1999.

Lafferty, J. Clayton. *Life Styles Inventory: LSI 1 Self-Development Guide*. Human Synergistics International, 2004.

Le Gun, Ursula. *The Wizard of Earthsea*. Bantam Books, 1975.

Maslow, Abraham H. *Toward a Psychology of Being*. John Wiley and Sons, Inc., 1968.

Miller, William A. *Your Golden Shadow*. Harper and Row Publishers, Inc. 1989.

Remen, M.D., Rachel Naomi. *My Grandfather's Blessings*. Riverhead Books, 2000.

Tharp, Twyla. *The Creative Habit: Learn It and Use It for Life*. Simon and Schuster, Inc., 2003.

RELATIONSHIP-BASED LEADERSHIP

Bridges, William. *Transitions*. Addison-Wesley Publishing Company, Inc., 1980.

Buckingham, Marcus and Curt Coffman. *First, Break All the Rules*. Simon and Schuster, 1999.

Flaherty, James. *Coaching: Evoking Excellence in Others*. Butterworth Heinemann, 1999.

Rogers, Carl R.. *On Becoming a Person*. Houghton Mifflin Company, 1961.

Rusk, Tom and Patrick D. Miller. *The Power of Ethical Persuasion*. Viking, 1993.

Salmon, Moshe. *Single Session Therapy*. Jossey-Bass Publishers, 1990.

Stone, Douglas, Bruce Patton and Sheila Heen. *Difficult Conversations*. Penguin Books, 1999.

Whitmore, John. *Coaching for Performance*. Nicholas Brealey Publishing, 2002.

TEAM DEVELOPMENT

Dyer, William. *Team Building*. Addison-Wesley Publishing Company,

Inc., 1987.

Reddy, W. Brendan, Editor. *Team Building: Blue Prints for Productivity and Satisfaction.* NTL Institute for Applied Behavioral Science, 1988.

Shonk, James. *Working in Teams.* Amacom, 1987.

Tuckman, Bruce. *Developmental Sequence in Small Groups. Psychological Bulletin* (Number 63, 1965, pp. 384-399).

VERSATILITY

Goleman, Daniel. *Working with Emotional Intelligence.* Bantam Books, 1998.

Hersey, Paul. *The Situational Leader.* Center for Leadership Studies, 1997.

Kaplan, Robert E. *Forceful Leadership and Enabling Leadership: You Can Do Both.* Center for Creative Leadership, 1996.

INDEX